Waiting
on the
Next Miracle

JEN WEIR

Never doubt your faith. Ever.
God's got you. Always.

ISBN 979-8-88832-064-8 (paperback)
ISBN 979-8-88943-007 0 (hardcover)
ISBN 979-8-88832-065-5 (digital)

Christian Faith Publishing
832 Park Avenue
Meadville, PA 16335
www.christianfaithpublishing.com

Printed in the United States of America

March 27, 2021. A normal Saturday for our family. Running around the house, yelling at the kids to get their stuff ready, loading the jeep with ski gear, grabbing coffee and a few snacks. Chaos.

Weston had his best buddy, Reid, over to celebrate his eighth birthday, so we had to run him down the road to his house. He was going skiing with his dad and sister that day as well. We told them we'd see them all up on the mountain.

Thirty minutes later, we were through town and on our way to the hill. Our search-and-rescue alert sounded; we were being called out to help recover a body. We weren't going to respond, just carry on with our day as planned. After a few minutes, we looked at each other and decided we better go help.

I texted Reid's dad and asked if he would meet us to take the kids up to the ski hill and we'd meet up with them after we responded. He agreed. We turned around and headed back to town, pulling off on the side of the road to wait. We saw them crest the hill.

The next thing I remember is waking up in the ICU four days later. Reid's dad (who is a fabulous ENT) was there, holding my hand to tell me what happened.

After we saw them crest the hill, my husband pulled out onto the road to turn around and meet them. Between the sun poking over the hill and the blind spots in the jeep, he never saw the semi. It was traveling the speed limit and hit us broadside.

Tyler, 35

Tyler John Weir was a man among men and said what he thought whether you liked it or not. He was born January 20, 1986, in Spokane, Washington, to Jaqueline Marshall and Ralph Weir. Tyler grew up surrounded by sisters, which just made him tougher. He attended St. Mary's private Catholic school until high school, where he attended and graduated from Gonzaga Prep.

Tyler's adventurous spirit led him to Bozeman, Montana, where he enrolled in mechanical engineering and ROTC. It was in Bozeman that Tyler met the love of his life, Jen, when he was nineteen. Jen was ready to get married, but Tyler made her wait four years and proposed right before leaving for Air Force Basic Training in December of 2008.

Tyler attended schools in Texas and Arkansas and then made a quick trip back to Montana in August of 2009 to marry his girl and whisk her off to his first duty station in Little Rock. In May 2011, the couple welcomed their first child. Wyatt was born in Little Rock and spent his first year of life in the South. In 2012, Tyler was able to transfer to the Montana Air National Guard in Great Falls, Montana. Tyler landed a job, and they welcomed their second child, Weston, in March of 2013. Wakely came as a surprise in July of 2014.

Tyler loved being outdoors hunting, hiking, cutting wood, working, finding sheds, and camping with his family. He was an active member of Cascade County Search and Rescue and Great Falls Ski Patrol. Tyler lived to help others and was always going above and beyond in all areas of his life, whether it was fixing a broken C-130 engine or talking one of his kids down after a bad day. Two days after the wreck, Tyler was awarded National NCO of the year in the Air National Guard. It had been decided internally the day before the wreck and announced two days after. Tyler never knew. No matter what he did, Tyler gave his all and will be missed every single day by those of us who knew him and loved him.

Wyatt, 9

Wyatt John Weir, aka Chatterbox, was a cowboy. He was born to his doting parents on May 31, 2011, in Little Rock, AR. He spent his first year hanging with mom down in the hot South. When he was a year old, Wyatt and his family got the okay to head back north to Montana.

Wyatt grew up surrounded by family who loved and adored him, and he was quickly followed by cousins and siblings. Weston was born when Wyatt was almost two, and Wakely came right after he turned three. He was the best big brother they ever could have asked for.

From the time he could dress himself, Wyatt loved dressing up in superhero costumes, and he wore them everywhere! Eventually, superheroes gave way to his true inner cowboy. Wyatt was a steer rider and got thumped every time, but he always wanted to do it again. He was an expert gopher slayer with his BB gun; he could pitch a baseball like a pro; he was super excited to hunt this year; he loved riding his horse and hiking and camping. But Wyatt most loved starting, building, and cooking over fires, and he was pretty amazing at it. Wyatt was fearless; nothing scared that boy.

Wyatt attended Our Lady of Lourdes Catholic School from pre-K through this year when he was a fourth grader. He never loved school, but he tolerated it and was slowly learning how it applied to real life.

I have no doubt my boy would have gone on to do something amazing with his life. Wyatt, we miss you every single day, and the world will be a little darker without your goofy grin in it.

Mom, Weston, and Wakely

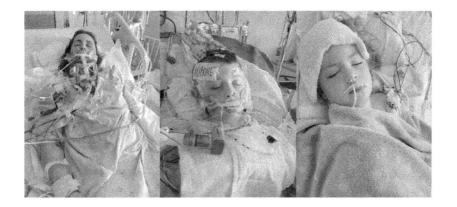

I was hooked up to all the wires and was still quite out of it between the meds and my head injury. I was told that I had suffered two collapsed lungs, a lacerated liver, a dissected aorta, and about sixteen rib fractures.

I was informed that Wakely and Weston had been life-flighted to Seattle after they were stabilized in Great Falls, which took quite some time. The prognosis for both was not good. I was getting updates while I was in the ICU, which didn't do much considering my mental state at the time. I was in ICU for nine days before I was transferred to rehab, against my will. My only thought was, *Get to Seattle*, but the doctors insisted I go to rehab first to ensure I could take care of myself. After three days, they agreed I was good enough and discharged me.

I finally got home. I walked in and bawled. Everything was the same as when we had left that Saturday morning. I felt my boys' overwhelming presence.

By this time, I was aware that Wakely had regained consciousness but still had a long road ahead of her. The last I had heard from the doctors in Seattle, Weston was considered very critical, and his brain had been severely damaged.

That Saturday, two weeks after the wreck, I went to the funeral home to say my last goodbyes. I walked in and saw them both lying in coffins. They looked so beautiful, just like they were napping. I cried and kissed them both one last time. I gave the director the go-ahead to let the rest of the family in to see them. I arranged for viewings for the two of them individually for friends and filled out the paperwork for cremation.

The next day, I flew to Seattle with my mom. Excitement filled me to see my other two babies, and I was full of thoughts planning the funerals—something I never dreamed of doing at the age of thirty-six.

Yes, this is a very sad story. But it's also an amazing story. The last year and a half has been filled with miracles. A lot of them. That's what this story is really about—waiting on the next miracle.

Miracles

Three of Us Survived

All five of us should have gone home that day. That semi hit our jeep traveling at sixty-five miles per hour. I have often thought, *If only it was just a regular vehicle*. But I know that would've been worse. The semi driver was, thankfully, only minimally injured. Had it been a pickup, car, or SUV that hit us, injuries to the other occupants would have been much more severe.

Instead, it was just us. Once we were hit, we rolled down an embankment. Our ENT friend's kids watched the whole incident happen. He was first on the scene. A neurologist from the hospital (whom I've come to know as a saint of a man) was also right there and used the knife on his key chain, which he had planned on removing but never did, to cut us out of the jeep. Had we spent any more time in the vehicle, we would not have survived. The fact that we were all in the ER within twenty-five minutes of the accident is a miracle.

I received a message from a gal from Wyoming whose husband was a doctor. They had been passing by at the time of the wreck. There were countless other "coincidental" medical professionals and first responders present at the time of impact. It is thanks to them, the quick response from the Belt EMS, fire department, and Jesus that we were taken from the jeep alive.

An EMT from Belt went so far as to have her husband go back to the jeep to find the kids' blankies. She took them home, washed them, and had them at the hospital the next day so that my brother could take them to Seattle with him. It doesn't seem big, but it was huge. Wakes and Weston have always loved those blankies and still do to this day.

We were blessed with help from people full of love. The medic on the helicopter who took Weston to the hospital from the scene was a true angel who said,

> The Mercy Flight team is thinking of you and most especially Weston, Wakely, and Jen. It was our honor and privilege to have been able to help in the care for them. I was the medic on the helicopter that brought Weston in. I have two sons, six and eleven. On that day, I had another son, Weston. We talked to him and let him know "it's okay, buddy." We reassured him on the love of his family. I know he heard us. I hope he heard the voice of his loving father talking to his son.

An oncology nurse also reached out to me:

Hi, Jen,

> I have always wanted to reach out to you but didn't know when I should. I feel deep in my heart that I wanted to share with you my story.
>
> I was headed to Billings for a shopping weekend. I typically stop at a quick Starbucks but chose to stop at the Homestead in Cascade, which delayed me forty-five minutes. If I didn't do this, I would have missed the accident.
>
> I was one of the first few on the scene. When I pulled over, they asked if I could help. I grabbed my kit from my car, and when I got down the hill, the guy handed me Wakely. I had no idea there were children in the vehicle. Being a mother myself, my heart sank, but adrenaline kicked in. I never left Wakely's side. I continued to check her pulse and rubbed her hand so she could hear my voice. I stayed with her along with

another man. When Mercy Flight showed, they asked me a bunch of questions, and I gave Miss Wakes oxygen and carried her on the backboard. I heard that they needed a blanket for Wes, which I grabbed from my vehicle.

I want you to know this has forever changed my life too. I have been in intensive therapy because that day forever changed me. I held your oldest son's hand and told him he was going to be with the amazing man upstairs. He looked peaceful, and I know God had him. The memories of this day forever changed me. One day I would love to meet you and the family, and I hope you know you will always hold a special place in my heart, and your children were never alone. God wanted me there that day, and it's amazing how one decision changed my whole life.

You are so brave and so strong I can't imagine how much you have to deal with. Just know we were there and forever will be your support system.

Family and friends were notified and told it didn't look good for us. They went so far as to discuss donating Weston's organs if they couldn't stabilize him for the flight to Seattle. It took a long time to get Wakely's breathing stable. I'm not exactly sure how I fared after—my best friend told me the first time she saw me, she wasn't so sure I was going to pull through.

Just a few months ago, over a year after the accident, I was talking to the kids' neurologist (he was the man on the scene who cut us out of the jeep). He was telling Wakely how strong her momma was. I brushed him off, and then he told me that after they got me out of the car and moved me to the road, I woke up and kept trying to get back into the jeep to get my kids. He said they had to take turns holding me back while the other tended to the kids.

Regardless, we all made it to the emergency room in Great Falls, where they did all they could for us.

Finally, the kids were stable enough to fly to Seattle. My sister hopped on the plane with Wakely, and my sister-in-law got on the first plane to Seattle from Spokane. I was left in Great Falls with my mom, stepdad, and sisters-in-law. Shortly after, both of my brothers flew to Seattle as well. I've always felt blessed to have my family, but now it's beyond words.

The staff at the hospital was so supportive. In the words of my mom, "They were great huggers and good criers—fully invested in Jen's recovery and the kids."

We Were in the Wreck as a Family

I know this seems like an odd fact to consider a miracle, but I'm grateful we were all together that day. The boys left this earth with the rest of their family by their sides. Had it just been Tyler and the kids, receiving the call would have killed me. Instead, I had four days of a coma and months of recovery to work through, which I will forever be grateful for, as I came to terms with our new life. I also had Wakely's and Weston's recovery to face and assist in. I can only imagine the anguish my family and Tyler's family had to deal with when they received the news. God knew that in order for me to come out stronger, I would need work to keep me busy.

One other small mercy, if you want to call it that, is that Tyler and Wyatt were the ones that got to go. I know how hard it was for me to say goodbye and lay them to rest. I know without a shred of doubt that had it been me and Wakes or me and Wes, Tyler and Wyatt would never have been at peace knowing they were left behind. By no means did Tyler love me more, nor was I stronger than him, yet I know that putting me in the ground would have broken him.

We had just recently rearranged the kids in the back seat. By all accounts, Wakely should have been sitting where Wyatt was sitting. At the time of the wreck, she was safely over on the passenger side.

Had she gone to heaven and Wyatt stayed, he would have been a broken little boy.

These are things I never would've considered had I not lived them. I still hate that the three of us are still here and not with our boys in eternity. All I can figure is that we're not done yet. Tyler and Wyatt both lived so big their entire lives. They both would've gladly sacrificed themselves for us, and they did. I can only imagine the fun, peace, and glory they are experiencing right now. The light and legacy they left has blown my mind repeatedly. It's now up to us to carry the torch forward and do as much good here as we can before we are finally called home.

Prayer

Immediately after the wreck, the praying began. My coworkers and the kids' teachers gathered at the school to pray and receive the updates. Our ENT friend went to the school to keep everyone on pace as the situation changed. From the start, it looked like none of us were going to make it. Then things would change for the better for one of us, then fall again. I've talked to my friends about this, and they said it was horrible, not knowing if we were going or staying. After several hours, they finally learned we were all stable, but there was much unknown as to our prognosis. Again, I'm so thankful I was unconscious for all this. My family was in the hospital as soon as they could get there.

Friends and family began praying. People I had never met, and will likely never meet, began praying. Prayers have not stopped to this day. We are living proof that prayer is a powerful weapon. Always has been and always will be.

Due to the immense outreach my family began to receive, my sister-in-law started a Facebook page so that everyone interested could follow our journey. As of today, there are nearly ten thousand people who are a part of our community. They are so full of love and support for us. It is truly amazing.

Peace

When I was brought out of my coma and told what had happened, I cried but did not lash out, scream, or fight it like everyone expected. Instead, I cried and was filled with an overwhelming sense of peace. I knew my guys were okay and happy. I knew we were going to be okay. I have tried to describe this peace to my family, but I just can't. God placed it on my heart, that's all I know.

I was telling this to Wakely's therapist the first time I met her. She had a profound thought. She asked me where I thought our souls went when we were in a coma. I said I had no idea. She suggested that perhaps my soul was able to interact with Tyler and Wyatt while I was unconscious, which I had never considered. Maybe that was why I was at such peace with everything. Maybe I knew at a soul level that we were *all* just fine. I won't be sure until I see them again, but I know that peace has never wavered a millimeter.

When I was still in the hospital, I repeatedly argued with my mom that the boys were fine at home. I would ask her to get my phone so I could call Tyler. I even did call him once and left a message. In my drug-induced and TBI-damaged brain, Tyler and Wyatt were perfectly fine at home. I knew they were dead, but I figured they could just hang around the house. They were still with us. My mom would get frustrated with me and say, "Jen, Tyler is not at home. Where is he?" I responded with, "I know, Mom, but I know he's fine at home."

This went on for a couple of days. Finally, I gave up on her busting me out to take me home to see my boys. It's been almost a year since the wreck, so I've had a lot of time to think about this. I believe this goes along with that feeling of peace I have. No, my boys were not just fine in our physical home. They were perfectly fine in their heavenly home. For as defiant and argumentative as I was with my mom, this is the only conclusion I have been able to come to. I already knew they were home, and, to this day, I anxiously await to join them in paradise.

Medical Intervention

Followed by the immediate rescue response that transpired after the wreck, the continued medical support and intervention at the hospital ensured that we would survive.

Weston underwent immediate surgery to get his lungs working again and save him from his ruptured spleen. A large portion of his skull was removed to prevent further damage from the swelling that took place once he arrived in Seattle.

Wakely's breathing was stabilized in Great Falls, and I was told it took quite some time. A bolt was put in her head to monitor the pressure. Half of her head was shaved in preparation for a possible craniectomy. My sister told me she had to fight the nurses in Seattle not to shave her entire head. They thought that would be easier than cleaning all the blood and debris out of her hair. My sister stood her ground and tediously worked through every centimeter of her beautiful long blond hair to salvage it.

My lungs were reinflated, my liver and brain were examined, and a stent was placed inside my dissected aorta. Nothing could be done for my ribs, of course.

Wakely Woke Up

The day after the wreck, Wakely woke up and looked around and then was immediately put back into a medically induced coma so as not to overstress her injured brain.

The next day, they brought her out of the coma, and my sister prayed with her that night. At the end of the prayer, Wakely weakly said, "Amen." Her first word since the wreck.

I Stood My Ground

When I first arrived in Seattle, I was ushered into a conference room where the neurologist gave me a bleak prognosis of Weston's recovery. He had not only suffered a severe TBI, he had also experienced multiple strokes in the hospital caused by clots coming out of his stretched carotid artery. These strokes went undetected for some time. The doctor said the TBI, which left only a piece of his brain the size of a walnut undamaged, was more than he could recover from, but then add in the strokes and it would be nearly impossible.

Finally, I was taken to his room and saw my precious boy lying there. He was covered in bandages, had tubes going and coming everywhere, and looked so broken. Another doctor came into the room. He looked at me and said, "You're going to have to decide."

I replied, "What?"

"You're going to have to decide when to take him off life support."

I was still in my own TBI and medical stupor and was very confused. "Why do I need to decide that?"

"Because he is not going to make it. You are just prolonging it."

"My boy is right there. He is going to be okay."

"No, he will not."

Finally, my sister stepped in. "Doctor, do you have kids?"

"Yes, older kids."

"Any kids his age?"

"Grandkids, yes."

"And what would you do if it was one of them lying here?"

"Um, I don't know."

"Then don't you stand there and tell my sister that she is going to have to decide when to end her kid's life."

He left the room after that.

The thing that got me about this entire encounter was that my boy was there. He was alive. He shouldn't have been, but he was. That peace I mentioned earlier was going strong; I knew he would be just fine. It would take time and a lot of healing from God, but he would be just fine. From that point on, I was in a constant battle with all the doctors who only saw the injured patient and not the feisty, healthy, strong boy I knew. I fought for him every step of the way and will continue to.

Weston's Guts Were Healthy

Several weeks into his hospital stay, Weston suddenly stopped pooping. Despite laxatives and meds, the little boy was showing no sign of pooping. They decided to do an explorative surgery, going through the same large incision he received when his spleen was removed. It had just begun to heal.

Prior to the late-night surgery, the surgeon came in and told me they expected to find injured and dead tissue in his intestines. They said they would have to remove all the unhealthy tissue and to brace for a large portion of his intestine to be removed, which would require a colostomy bag for the rest of his life.

I went back to the Ronald McDonald House scared but praying. It was just another prediction from the doctors who always seemed to run with the worst-case scenario.

Late that night, my phone rang. The surgeon was calling to update me. Weston's intestines looked perfectly healthy. As they worked their way through them inch by inch, they found where it had simply turned inward on itself—likely a by-product of the splenectomy. They smoothed it out, sewed him back up, and the boy hasn't had a problem pooping since. Something that could have been horrendous turned out to be nothing much at all.

Breathing Tube Removed

On May 3, 2021, the doctors started talking about potentially removing Weston's breathing tube, something I'd been praying for and knew Weston desperately wanted. By May 5, the doctors were no longer confident in removing his tube. They suggested we just schedule a tracheostomy, believing he did not have the strength or ability to breathe on his own.

Momma bear came out in full force. I was not about to schedule another surgery without giving him a chance. They advised against it, but I was adamant. On May 6, an entire team gathered in his room, ready to pounce and stick the tube back in once he failed to maintain his breath. The doctor had already been in to tell me that she did not encourage me and pushed once more for the scheduling of the surgery. I stood my ground, prayed, and asked everyone else to pray.

The time came. They removed the tube, and everyone stood ready to move. Weston coughed a couple of times and took a breath. Then another. After an hour, they agreed he was indeed ready to have his tube out. They monitored him for the next forty-eight hours, believing the tube would need to be replaced. Guess what? My God is good.

Wakely Made It to Her Kindergarten Graduation

From the very beginning of seeing Wakely in Seattle, I prayed she would make it home in time for her kindergarten graduation. It's a small thing, but in the realm of getting our lives back on track, it was a really big thing.

She spent several weeks in the hospital before she was sent to rehab at Seattle Children's. When we first arrived, they told us to plan on a month of rehab, which would have made attending graduation very unlikely.

After one week of rehab, they said she was ready to go home! We checked her out of the hospital and took her back to the Ronal McDonald House. Before I could let her leave Seattle, I insisted she go see the ocean—one fun thing for her to remember in a place she had experienced nothing but pain. It was cold and rainy, but the beach was amazing. We walked along, picking up shells and throwing rocks in the water. Afterward, we went back to the house and enjoyed her "jailbreak" sword-horse (unicorn) cake.

The next morning, we went to the airport and loaded up onto the private jet to take my girl back to Montana. I stayed with her for a few days before I went back to Seattle to be with my boy. My mom stayed with Wakely as she slowly integrated back into a school routine. It was still about three weeks until graduation, so she was able to spend time with her classmates, and they had time to overcome the excitement of seeing her again.

I flew back to Montana for the funerals and her graduation. She looked so beautiful in her little cap and gown, standing up there grinning with the rest of her class. Her daddy would've been so proud to see his little girl up there. I know he and Wy were right there beside me in the pew.

Embrace the Journey

I can't tell you how many times I've wished I could just wake up five years from now. See my happy, healed kids, be married to my second soul mate, and not have to deal with any more of the difficult days.

Where's the growth in that? I quickly realized the journey is where everything happens. Where the miracles happen. Where the dark, bottomed-out days happen. Where overcoming and climbing all those mountains happen.

Although the journey is a rough one, I'm grateful for every day I get to experience. Every day that brings something new. Every day I learn just how strong I am. Every day I witness my kids living with the grit their daddy instilled in them.

I have embraced the journey and am seeing it for what it is. A miracle.

Private Jet

An amazing family in Great Falls contacted me shortly after the wreck to offer their private jet for our use to go back and forth to Seattle. What a blessing that was! My mom and I flew to Seattle originally on it, Wakely and Weston each flew home on it, and we were able to use it a couple of other times.

To have the ability to fly without other passengers and without the airport lines when you are in the midst of the biggest grief storm of your life was truly beyond words. I can never thank this family enough. Small acts of kindness go such a long way. Please always do what you can to help others going through hard spots.

Weston's Skull Replacement Went Smoothly

After what seemed like eons, the day arrived for Weston to have his skullcap put back on. It had spent a couple of months in a freezer at Harborview Medical Center. I was so excited to see my boy whole again.

The day finally came when the doctors felt comfortable with the shunt doing its job keeping the fluid at a safe level. Up to this point, he had a bulbous protrusion of fluid on the right side of his head where the skull was gone. It was soft, and he had to wear a helmet when doing anything to protect his brain.

The day of the surgery, they told me and my sister that it would take four to six hours, so we planned on exploring the area and waiting for the call. An hour and a half later, my phone rang. The surgeons were ready to meet with me. I panicked at first but was assured everything went perfectly and much quicker than they had expected. We headed back to the hospital and waited until they wheeled him back to his room from recovery.

He had to wear horrible rough gauze around his head for several days to keep the swelling down, but even with it I could see the beautiful round shape of his head once again. When the gauze came off, there were still staples all over his scalp, but his head was perfect, and he looked like Weston again.

Weston Ate Pudding

Once his skull was secure, he was cleared to move to the rehab floor from ICU. Up to this point, he had been surviving on only what went through his feeding tube. My sister and I had snuck him drops of water on the toothbrush sponge, for the simple fact that neither of us could imagine not having anything on your tongue for months.

Speech therapists began working with him and testing the waters. They introduced chocolate pudding, and that boy's life changed. They would give him tiny little bites to ensure he wouldn't choke. The boy wanted it all. He knew his speech therapist's voice, so as soon as she walked in and said hello, he was ready to do whatever he had to in order to get the pudding.

Before we left Seattle, they performed a swallow test. He passed with flying colors and was cleared for thick liquids. That was it. But Momma needed her boy to eat steak. Once we were home, we slowly started introducing more and more pureed foods and then worked up to solids. Within a couple of months, Weston was surviving on home-cooked meals, and we mailed the pump for the feeding tube back. One year later, he tells me exactly what he wants to eat multiple times per day. If you ever think you're a short-order cook for your kids now, try accommodating a hungry nine-year-old boy in a wheelchair. It never ends.

Weston Was Home for Wakely's Birthday

All Wakely wanted for her seventh birthday was for her brother to be home. God answered that little girl's prayers, and Weston was discharged from the hospital on July 13, 2021—sixteen weeks after being admitted. Wakely's birthday is the twenty-third. We had the pool rented, friends invited, and a doughnut tower ready for the party.

Unfortunately, the day of her birthday, I received a call from the doctor. Weston's electrolytes were dangerously out of balance due to the formula he was ingesting. I was advised to get him to the emergency room immediately. I dutifully took him, praying it was a quick fix and we'd be done by party time. Turns out, the ER takes forever, and then they decided to admit him in order to administer IVs until his electrolytes were where they needed to be. I was devastated. Not only would Weston miss Wake's birthday but so would I.

God had other plans and sent my angel friend to the hospital. She volunteered to stay with Weston so that I could go to the party, run home to grab an overnight bag, and then return to the hospital. Everyone needs at least one friend like that.

Wakes was bummed her brother didn't actually get to attend her party, but she had a fabulous time anyway. Four days later, Weston was discharged.

Weston Slept

The entire time in the hospital, Weston rarely slept. He napped very seldom during the day, and at night they pumped him full of meds to sleep. It didn't work. That boy was so exhausted. How was he supposed to heal when he couldn't sleep?

The day he got home, I set him on the couch, and he fell asleep. He slept that night and every night after. All he needed was his own bed and the home he knew.

Weston Was Weaned off Meds

We left Seattle with an entire cooler full of medication. It was constant administering throughout the day and night. They were a lot to deal with on top of everything else. I'm not a big fan of meds, so I started figuring out what we could start weaning. He was on meds for blood pressure, which was constantly high in the hospital, but once we were home, it went right back to where it should be.

He was on medication for a host of other issues, many I cannot remember today. He now has one medication given three times per day for muscle spasticity. That's it. Oh, and fish oil. A whole lot of oil for his brain. His body is taking care of itself now. God is good.

Weston Moved Past Midline

For months after the wreck, Weston could only look right. His eyes were directed to the right, and his head was turned sharply to the right. We were told this was due to the brain injury, that he may never be capable of sight to the left.

Enter our tribe. While I was at DC, accepting Tyler's airman of the year award, the kids stayed with our ENT friend and his family. He had been researching on his own and rigged up a pair of goggles with electrical tape over the right half of the lenses. The theory was that if Weston wanted to see something, he would be forced to move his eyes to midline. He took it one step further and used an exercise band to secure Weston's head straight ahead in his wheelchair and stander. He would then let Weston box his hands just to give him a target to look at.

We also began using electrodes on the left side of neck, shoulders, and face, attempting to stimulate the muscles.

It wasn't instant success, but over time, Weston's eyes began to move to the middle more and more. His head began to slowly transition to the center. From there, he kept improving. Today, Weston can look in all directions and has amazing peripheral vision. He doesn't miss a thing, which sometimes comes back to bite me.

Weston Spoke

When we left Seattle, there was little hope (from their side) that Weston would ever speak again. He hadn't even mouthed a word. Once we got home, we had in-home therapists coming a few times a week. Miss Lori, his speech therapist, kind of took a liking to Weston. She worked diligently with him each time, trying to refamiliarize him with his body, his mouth in particular. They focused on very basic tasks such as moving his lips and tongue, and creating sensations in and around his mouth.

During this time, it was clear he could understand what we were saying to him, but he lacked the ability to respond. By the beginning of September, we were able to get him to say one word at a time. His first attempt was "Ni, Way"—("night, Wakes") when I was putting him to bed one night. Then, a few days later, he said, "Maaaa." He was crying at me when I was getting him dressed after a bath. I told him if he was going to make a noise that he should at least say something like "mom." He did just that. Each of these took everything he had to get a noise out.

Then, on September 18, I got him up, fed him some breakfast, and then wheeled him into the living room. Wakely was constantly trying to get him to talk and was always making him laugh. That morning, she got him to say "beer." I said, "Weston James! Why did you just say beer!" He replied with, "Because Wakely told me to." I completely lost it and started screaming with excitement. Wakely was completely clueless.

And, just like that, Weston was talking. He hasn't stopped yet. In fact, prior to the wreck, his nickname was Porkchop (Wyatt was Chatterbox). He has since adopted the nickname Chatterbox Porkchop and tells me that's why he *has* to talk. He wears me out, but I honestly *love* the sound of his little angelic voice, especially after not hearing it for so long. I feel like when Wyatt left earth, he thought it fitting to leave his propensity for talking with his little brother. I'm really grateful he did.

Weston's Blood Levels Were Perfect

As I mentioned before, Weston missed Wakely's birthday due to electrolyte imbalances. His calcium was extremely high (we almost didn't get to leave Seattle the day we had planned due to the levels), and his potassium was very low.

The doctors said the calcium was high because his bones were releasing calcium into his bloodstream due to lack of mobility. The potassium I blamed on his horrible diet fed through the tube.

The doctors in Seattle wanted to give him an infusion medication to force his bones to reabsorb the calcium, but it came with a host of horrible side effects. The doctor here wanted to avoid that medication if possible.

Instead, we had to get regular blood draws, which he absolutely hated, to monitor his blood levels. For two months, they progressively got a little better. In October, one month after switching entirely to real food, his blood levels were perfect. He hasn't had to have them checked again.

Weston's Hearing and Vision

In the hospital, I was told Weston would likely have limited hearing and sight. They were sure that his brain damage would hinder him significantly. A hearing test was performed shortly before we left, and he passed with flying colors. Once he started talking, he constantly yelled at me for being too loud. His hearing was not only intact, it was supersonic.

His eyesight was questionable for some time. He would watch us but not make eye contact. We were never sure what he was actually seeing. He seemed to have some blind spots in his field of vision, and he would guess at colors. As time went on, God continued to work on Weston. He can now see whatever he wants to in any direction and any angle. Last spring, he started nailing his colors, assuring us that color blindness was not part of his future.

Kidney Stones

In Seattle, the doctors discovered that Weston had several kidney stones—multiple small ones and one very large one. They blamed this on the calcium release from his bones due to the inactivity and were fairly concerned about them. Once we got home and met with an endocrinologist, he had a different opinion. He said there was no way the stones would form that quickly and believed they had existed prior to the wreck, but we were oblivious to them.

In August of 2021, he had orders to get an ultrasound of his kidneys done, and they were still there in all their glory. In May of 2022, we went to a urologist here. Going from the August ultrasound, he was quite worried about them. The doctor said that Weston could likely pass the smaller ones, but there was no way even a large grown man would be able to pass the large one; he suggested that surgery to remove them may be in order.

July of 2022, we went in for another ultrasound. The ultrasound tech was not able to find anything. The pediatrician called a couple of days later and confirmed the results—Weston no longer had any kidney stones present.

He may have passed them on his own, but not one single time did he ever talk about any discomfort of pain when urinating. I believe God took care of them, just like he has everything else in that little boy's life.

It Happened to Us

This may seem like a ludicrous idea to put in a book about miracles, but it needs to be said. Am I grateful we lost our guys and that our lives were turned upside down? No, I miss our life and them terribly. However, I am grateful it happened to us for the mere reason that if it wasn't us, it would have been somebody else.

The pain and loss we have experienced has been paralyzing at times, but I know it would be for someone else as well. I would much rather take that burden on myself than to watch someone I know and love, or even someone I've never met, go through it.

We had an amazing life, and it would be easy for me to ask God, "Why us?" But life is full of grace, and I have been surrounded with that grace and am able to look at everything and almost be grateful. Yes, I would give anything to hug each of them one more time; however, I know that both of them would be glad they were able to give up their lives for their family. I believe they knew before they were born that it was going to be a short ride, but they both willingly signed up because they knew how much good they would leave behind.

That is why they both lived so well and so hard; why they both shone so bright during their lives; why they both left an impact on everyone they met. They were both bigger than life, and now, almost a year and a half into it, I realize they are both bigger than death.

God graced me with a sense of stubbornness and grit that I've always had but have never had to harness to the extent I have since the wreck. With the healing of my kids, I have never backed down. The grieving has never fully broken me. My soul is so, so happy knowing where Tyler and Wyatt are, but my humanity misses them dearly.

I am grateful we were the ones who took this hit, simply because God had given us and continues to give us the tools we need to battle our way through. God is good, even when bad things happen. Let us learn through the trials and come out the other side stronger than before.

We Were Prepared

Over these last eighteen months, I've finally come to realize the true purpose of my life and why so many things happened.

I've never had an easy life. There's been a lot of good, but also a lot of hard and flat-out crap. But I wouldn't ask for another one. My parents had a tumultuous marriage until they divorced when I was fifteen, yet we had the best childhood I could ask for. Running around wild, riding horses, playing with our cousins, just living the way kids are supposed to live. Could it have been better? Absolutely. But it helped form me into the adult I have become. It made me strong, tough, and resilient.

I've always kind of drifted through life with no real direction. In high school, I dabbled with the idea of becoming a doctor, considered sports medicine, got to college, and changed my major to animal science, then to biotechnology, and finally settled on exercise physiology because it sounded kind of cool. (I highly advise young people to take some time off before going to college, to get to know who you truly are.)

I was accepted to grad school in Minnesota for cardiac rehab, but the tall drink of water I was dating proposed and left for the military, so I headed back home to work for my basketball coach on his ranch for eighteen months (same place I worked during college and high school). All that ranch work added to my grit and determination. Sitting in a swather for fourteen hours a day, calving all day long day in and day out through what seems like an endless winter, and building fences forges you into a pretty formidable individual.

We got married in 2009 and moved to AR—his duty station. We didn't particularly care for it, but we made the best of it for three years. We tried everything we could think of to get out. Tyler pursued SERE for the second time, after a ton of paperwork and begging. He made it through the selection course, and then, for reasons beyond our understanding, the cadre decided to not allow him and a couple of other individuals to move on to the next part of training. An unprecedented move. We were devastated. Not only was that what we saw as our only chance, Wyatt and I had to be by ourselves for two weeks in a place where I knew no one. Because God knows the whole story, it turns out that wasn't our only chance to leave AR. I found out from a friend in MT that the guard unit was going to be transitioning to C-130s—the plane Tyler had been working on for years. He palace-chased and moved from active duty to a full-time guardsman, back in MT!

While we were in AR, I realized being a housewife was not my calling and decided to pursue my strength and conditioning certification and, in the meantime, fell into a freelance writing gig that continues to this day. Had we not spent that time in AR alone, I know our marriage would not have become as strong as it did, we would not have developed the resilience we did, and I may not have fallen into the rabbit hole of all things physiology, health, and training.

After AR, we transferred to MANG and moved to Great Falls. Found a house; Tyler worked on the hill; I continued writing and raising three kids (when Wakes was born, Wyatt had just turned three and Wes was fifteen months—so it was insane).

The year Wy started kindergarten, Tyler deployed for five months. He left in October, came home in March, and I was totally on my own all winter with three little kids. Didn't know a soul in GF. But we made it. Actually, Tyler was gone a lot for work over the course of our marriage. He was off galivanting through the globe, and I was home momming.

Five years ago, the school needed a gym teacher, so I decided to give it a whirl. I'm not a teacher, but I like exercise, so I went with it. Three years ago, I took a chance and started an online health and fitness business. It's done wonderful.

Where am I going with all this babble? Despite the aimlessness and random direction my life has seemed to have taken, it has all prepared me for the here and now, to get through what has hit our family and help this little boy make a full recovery.

God did not orchestrate the wreck, but he knew it was coming and that I'd need every experience he could give me to make it through and bring *good* out of it.

Growing up on a ranch, playing sports, doing hard manual labor jobs, experiencing my parents getting divorced, having poor self-esteem and a competitive nature, never knowing how things would work out, falling in love with lifting weights and ridiculous physical challenges—all of that has physically and mentally prepared me for what I'm doing now.

Tyler being gone so much prepared me for life as a truly single mom. Ranch work made me strong, independent, and gave me the ability to MacGyver any situation.

The natural ability I've always had to geek out over the human body, especially neurology, fascia, nutrition, and the muscular system, has allowed me to consume as much information as possible to help Weston. Not to mention the loads of information I already had in my brain.

My stubbornness, fighter's heart, and pigheadedness has also been a huge player in my life and continues to be. Thank you, God.

Finally, my knack for dreaming big—I've always wanted to open an in-person fitness space. But now the plan has shifted to a pediatric neuro-rehab facility here in Great Falls. Ultimately, I believe that is what's supposed to come out of all this. Local help for families in our part of the country—not a single kid should ever slip between the cracks due to finances, lack of knowledge, or insufficient resources.

The fact that we had to look for rehab in Arizona, Chicago, Baltimore, and finally Spokane is insane, as is the fact that I've had to do all the research to figure out how best to help Wes because the hospital sent us home with nothing. They had given up on him.

That is not acceptable; our kids deserve better. Our families deserve better.

Weston has essentially been the guinea pig, and I've been taking notes. Everything that has helped him will help others, which is what we love to do.

I don't know if any of this makes sense, but just know we will never be done with our work here until it's time for us to join our guys.

Wakely's Healing

Wakely had quite a bit of physical healing to do; however, most of what she had to conquer was emotional and spiritual. Her entire world was flipped upside down. Losing her daddy was absolutely devastating to her. Add in that her biggest brother was no longer with us and her other brother now significantly different, and she had a lot of work to do.

Several months after the wreck, she wasn't the happy little girl she used to be. She understandably had attachment, trust, and, I would say, abandonment issues. I was gone a lot to be with Weston, so I relied heavily on my amazing momma to be with my baby girl.

Wakes started seeing a therapist the fall after the wreck, but it didn't seem to make much of a difference. Then, the following spring, we had a woman reach out to us. She was a Godsend. After a few months of visiting with her on a weekly basis, Wakes is back to her crazy self. She's still different than she used to be. But she's able to love, be vulnerable, and trust again.

She has been a pivotal part of Weston's healing. The most resilient little sister he could ever ask for. Wakes still misses her daddy and brother terribly, and sometimes we have a good cry together. I've told her multiple times that she has gone through the hardest thing in her life she'll ever have to deal with. She can do anything in her life; nothing will stop that girl.

My Physical Healing

Along with my spiritual healing was my physical healing. I was in rough shape after I woke up in the hospital. I have never been in that much pain in my life. Every breath was excruciating.

The hardest part for me was my physical limitations. I have always been a very active, tough lady. There wasn't much I couldn't do. After the stent and being strapped with multiple rib fractures, I was very restricted on what I could do. There was no cardiac rehabilitation after I was released, so I took it upon myself and what I knew about the human body to get my heart working like it was supposed to. I covered a lot of miles in Seattle trying to regain some measure of stamina.

The broken ribs prohibited me from anything but a slow shuffle. I never knew bones could take that long to heal. In the months following the wreck, I lost about twenty pounds, most of which was muscle. But I worked at it every day.

By the middle of June, I had begun to incorporate some jogging back into my routine. It was slow and it hurt, but I was doing it. Tyler and I had signed up for the Glacier half-marathon the previous fall, so I went ahead and ran-walked it with his number pinned to my bum.

A week later, I was back in Seattle with my sister. We were to the point where we could get Wes out of bed and put him in a wheelchair for an hour or two. The only problem was we had to use a Hoyer lift to get him in and out of bed unless the male nurse was on shift. There wasn't one female nurse there who would attempt to lift him. The lift was a pain in the keester, so I decided to see if I could lift him. I wasn't sure since I was so weak and sore still, but I had my sister for backup. I lifted that little boy out of bed and set him in his chair that day and have every day since.

Cubby

The weekend before the wreck, we went to my sister's house to celebrate all the March birthdays in the family. This included Weston, a couple of his cousins, and his uncle. It was chaotic and fun like all our family gatherings are.

My sister had just gotten a new puppy. Her name was Tula, an adorable black bundle of fur. Naturally, I fell in love. I mentioned to Jes how stinking cute her pup was, and she casually mentioned that the gal had one more left. Tyler looked at me, narrowed his eyes, and said, "Jen, no."

I said, "Oh, come on, honey. We can just look at him." Tyler shook his head and walked away. My sister had already texted her neighbor, who just happened to be passing by with the pup in her car. She stopped by and unloaded the dog. We were all outside enjoying the weather and the kids running around. The pup, which was a retriever-border-collie mix, lumbered around and sniffed, then walked over and lay on Tyler's shoes.

Tyler looked at me with his shy, goofy grin and said, "Maybe we need to take him home." I just about dropped to the ground. Tyler was always reining me in on animals, because I would have an entire farm on our place if I could. He kept me in check. For him to be the one to want to add another dog to the family was crazy!

So when we loaded up to head back to Great Falls, I had a big little furball on my lap. He looked like Ty (haha), big even as a puppy and so smart. We enjoyed his presence for that next week. The kids fought over what to name him; they all had their lists. Finally, I said we would name him Cubby, just so the poor guy could have a name. Tyler was smitten with him. I sent him pictures every day when I took the dogs for a walk. Little Cubby kept up with the big girls every time.

After the wreck, the ENT friend and his family took Cubby to their house to take care of him, so my parents weren't dealing with a puppy on top of everything else. By the time I saw him again, he had grown so much but was even smarter than before.

They started taking him to puppy classes and suggested perhaps using him as a service dog. I was able to find trainers just north of town and gave them a call. When I went to meet them with Cubby, he nailed everything they asked him to do. They told me he would be so easy to train and agreed to take him on. The husband also told me he was the first in line of the cars that were detoured around our wreck. He had been returning from a straight-through drive from Missouri. They were happy to help.

As of today, Cubby is learning everything he can with them and is excelling at it all. I'm not in the least bit surprised that Tyler would leave us with such a gift. The smartest (and one of the bigger dogs) I have ever seen is going to be taking care of his little boy. You were always the best Daddy, Ty.

Signs

Losing the boys left huge holes in our lives. Their big, vibrant, happy personalities were no longer part of our daily existence.

Within a few weeks of Wakes returning home, we came up with a few ways to know our guys were still watching out for us.

Every time a C-130 flew over (which happens very often since we live within five minutes of the guard base), Wakely decided it was her daddy saying, "I love you, baby girl." That has transitioned into him sharing his love with all of us each time one roars by.

Wyatt wore his cowboy hat with a big ol' feather, so feathers became his sign. You would not believe the love that boy has for us. The house is full of feathers we've found since the wreck. Not just plain, ugly feathers, but big beautiful hard-to-find feathers.

We know they are beyond happy where they are, but they have not forgotten about the rest of us waiting here to get home.

Soul-Searching

By all accounts, I am a different person now—a better person. I miss my guys terribly, yet I can only imagine how happy they are right now. I'm jealous of them every day for getting to go while the rest of us had to stay behind.

I was a widow at thirty-six. Would I ever find another love like I had with Tyler? I was so terribly lonely. I finally realized I wasn't looking for another guy. I was looking for love. That immense incredible love that Tyler had for me. I missed Wyatt's love, but thankfully God saw fit to leave me with two of my children. I had nothing to make up for the love lost when Tyler left. One dark day, I was lying in bed trying to get ready for sleep, crying my eyes out, talking to Tyler. All of a sudden, I felt it. I felt his love in all its strength. I wept harder. I had missed it for so long, when I finally took the time to sit down and receive it, it knocked me to my knees. It made me realize I had his love all along. Always had, always will. I don't need another man to attempt to give me something I will always have.

I've also gained an entirely new perspective on life. I was grateful for what I had before, but I'm beyond grateful for what I have now. This new life we have found ourselves in has the potential to be better than we can even imagine.

I do not lose my temper anymore. I have more patience than I ever dreamed possible. I love bigger, deeper, and harder than I ever have, which can be too intense for some people. I have given in fully to the "real" Jen, which means I say what's on my mind, I'm not scared to stand up to anyone who is not giving my kids what they need, I buy something if I want it now (after thirty-six years of spending very little money on myself, ever). I see the good in everything. I am not scared of anything. Life is short to begin with; once you experience a loss so big and nearly lose your own life in the process, you realize it's truly time to LIVE and to live well. I had no regrets when the boys left us, and I want to ensure I will have zero regrets when I leave this world.

Lastly, I had to reframe my way of thinking. I had to take what happened as a blessing. A blessing to walk through the fire. Just like wildfires leave destruction, they also bring amazing new growth the next spring, and the year after, and the year after. This fire I've walked through has allowed a rebirth of my soul. It has allowed me to find a whole new level of myself in Jesus. I have reached the end of my rope more times than I can count, but every time I found myself hanging on for dear life, there was Jesus reaching out his hand to pull me back up. He never left my side. He let me get burned, but he healed my wounds so now all I have are the scars to remind me of my strength.

My Soul Didn't Break

For me, this is one of the biggest miracles. By all accounts, it should have destroyed me. And it did, to a point. But it didn't break me.

When I was in the hospital, I just wanted to get home. When I finally walked through the door, it hit me like a freight train. I could feel them so strongly, memories flooded from everywhere. I cried. It was exactly where I needed to be.

My first task was to pick out clothes for the boys to be dressed in at the funeral home. I chose for Tyler a sweater, Western shirt, wranglers, and a bow tie because he always wore one when he dressed up. I sent his belt and his well-worn hunting cap. For Wyatt, I picked out his favorite Western shirt, his wranglers, belt, and his beloved felt hat he had just bought himself a few months earlier.

I sent the clothes to the funeral home and was told I need a bigger shirt for Tyler—his neck was too swollen for his regular shirt. So I went to North 40 and bought him a beautiful Western shirt and bought Wy a brand new pair of mocs—the last thing I will ever get to buy him.

That Saturday, two weeks after the wreck, I walked into the viewing room to say my final goodbye to my boys. As soon as I saw them, I started crying. I will never forget how peaceful they looked, like they were napping. My beautiful baby boy was lying there with his cowboy hat in his hands across his stomach. He had no marks. He was perfect. He would not have approved of his fancy hairdo, but other than that, he looked like he always had. I kissed my baby goodbye and moved on to his handsome daddy—the love of my life. He could have just been sleeping on the couch at home. Besides his large neck, he was perfect too. I kissed him goodbye and cried for a few more minutes before I allowed the rest of the family with me to come and say their goodbyes.

That was the last time I got to see them before they were cremated—the decision I had made while I was still in the hospital. I had no idea what to do for them, but Tyler and I had talked about it before, so I wasn't totally guessing. I had the funeral home remove their belts and keep Wy's hat, which still hangs in his room, and had them keep the rest of their clothes on them.

Next, I had to meet with the military people and funeral home about the funeral. I picked out the urns for my boy and my husband. I went to the cemetery and picked out and paid for four plots for our family. I designed Wyatt's footstone; the military took care of Tyler's for me. I never would have imagined at the age of thirty-six, I'd be burying my husband and son. No parent should ever have to bury their child. It's so backward.

Finally, in May, we had the funerals. We had a vigil on Friday night and a funeral mass on Saturday. I chose the boys' favorite possessions to display with their framed pictures and urns. For Wyatt, I chose his cowboy hat, his Packers football, and Packers jersey I had made for him with *Weir* on the back. For Tyler, I chose his hunting boots, his handmade knife my brother had made him, and his beloved ram skull that he'd found while hunting. After much deliberation, I settled on two songs—"The Ride" by Chris LeDoux and "If We Never Meet Again This Side of Heaven" by Johnny Cash.

I sat in the front pew with my family, held my rosary, and cried as I looked at what remained of my boys. I know I will see them again, but it seems like the rest of my time on this earth is going to take forever before I can be with them again. At the burial, a man offered to play the bagpipes for them. I asked him to play "Amazing Grace," and it was beautiful. They got a twenty-one-gun salute as a send-off. Officers from the base presented us with flags. Colonel Dahlin presented Wakely with a flag, and he wept as he spoke to her about her daddy and handed it over. The firing squad gave me the brass from their guns. The guard arranged for a C-130 to fly over—it carried their hunting packs, another flag for us, and the flag from the SAR building.

We finished with just the family. We all placed something in the urn box. I left Wyatt his favorite T-shirt and a bull-riding cross. For Tyler, I left the first wedding ring I had given him that was too big; I kept the one he actually wore. All the cousins put paper mustaches in for Wyatt because he always wore a fake one. We all took a shot of whiskey and poured some in with our boys, and then, together, we shoveled the dirt into the hole. We wanted to be the ones to lay them in their resting place.

Their unrealized goals and dreams fill my soul. I know how much good their losses have brought to the community, but I can't help but imagine how much more good they both could have given the world with their lives.

I am only still standing and moving forward today because of the miracle of grace. Without God by my side, there is no way I could have made it through all that. I know I will see them again one day, but my human self feels like it will be an eternity before I get to spend eternity with them.

House

About four years ago, right after Tyler got home from deployment, we started looking for a house outside of town. Actually, I had begun looking while he was still in the desert, but I hadn't found anything yet. After a ton of looking and several offers that fell through, we decided to build. We just needed land.

I managed to find five acres up on the hill, five minutes to the gates at the base with views of the mountains I had been dreaming about. It was affordable and had zero covenants—Tyler said no one was going to tell him what he could and could not do with his own land. We put in a low offer our realtor told us would likely insult the sellers. But they countered just a smidge higher, and we closed.

We spent the next couple of years making land payments. We didn't want to build before the land was paid off. Finally, we got to the point where we could talk to a contractor. I met with him and told him what we wanted and what our budget was. He nailed it and said he could start in September or October. We were stoked. But then things changed, and they were able to break ground in July of 2019.

We took the kids up regularly to see the progress of their new home. What an amazing experience, and the crew was phenomenal. On December 6, we moved into our forever dream home.

The whole family loved it up there. The kids missed the trees from our old house in town, but they soon found how much more fun you can have out in the country with gophers, pastures, and lots of gravel roads.

While the house itself was a blessing prior to the wreck, it was so much more after. We had designed a nice open layout with just a couple of stairs to get in. The old house was a split-level with narrow hallways. Had we still been there, we would've had to move before Weston came home from Seattle. Instead, all I had to do was have a good friend build a ramp in the garage and buy a new couch.

Weston thrived at home. His healing and progression accelerated.

On Pearl Harbor Day of 2021, the Tunnels to Towers Foundation paid off our mortgage. Talk about a miracle. Our SAR commander had submitted our story shortly after the wreck and was told within a day we would be taken care of. They started paying our mortgage in May and officially paid it off in December. Now the home Tyler and I built together will be mine until I join him. I am grateful Tyler and Wyatt were able to enjoy a full year on the "homestead"—they loved it here.

Weston Walks

They say it takes a village to raise a child. It also takes a village to get a child out of a wheelchair after a TBI.

In Seattle, they told me he would never walk. In fact, they told me had no feeling in his feet. I told them they were incorrect for the sheer fact that every time I picked dry skin off his feet (something moms do…at least this weird mom) and put lotion on them, he would kick at me. I was pretty sure a kid with zero feeling in his legs would not worry about mom playing with his toes.

So the quest began to get Weston out of his chair. We did the basic physical therapy of stretching and range of motion from the beginning. I used a massage gun on his legs in the hospital to keep blood flow moving along.

We went to a wonderful woman in Missoula who practiced the Feldenkrais Method, something I had read about in one of the many books I discovered after the wreck.

An amazing gal at the Peak in Great Falls did aquatic therapy with him for several weeks.

I found a place in town that offered hyperbaric treatment. He patiently endured about twelve treatments before we left for Spokane.

His Auntie Steph gave him a few massages, which he didn't seem to mind too bad.

Physical therapy at St. Luke's included more stretching and range of motion. Empire Therapy introduced gravity line therapy, which I began to include with our daily morning stretching.

Reiki healing came into play, and his momma prayed like she's never prayed.

As of today, August 25, 2022, I feel it coming. I know it's only a matter of time until his brain reconnects to his body and he starts moving. I feel it in my soul. It's a matter of the boy making up his mind that he *wants* to get out of his chair so we can light it on fire and run it over the buffalo jump—that's the plan he came up with.

In the last month, he has managed to master the kicking motion and asks anyone he knows to stand in front of his chair so he can kick them.

Every morning before he gets up, I stretch him, and he works hard to bend and straighten his legs. I'm adding resistance the stronger he gets.

He has been doing a ton of tall kneeling at PT, using a bench in front to support himself. His PT has him reaching, moving, and shooting baskets. His glutes and back are fully engaged.

He has not walked yet. But he's ready, and my momma heart feels it's almost time. He has even begun talking about "when he's walking"—it about makes my heart burst with joy. That boy is going to run and play and be a kid again. At Christmas, the bishop asked me if they think he'll get out of his chair. I simply told him that God and I do. He threw his head back, laughed, and clapped me on the shoulder. God is good, and he has my boy in the palm of his hand.

EMDR

EMDR, eye movement desensitization and reprocessing, is a psychotherapy treatment originally designed to alleviate the distress associated with traumatic memories. Guess what, I had a few of those. Not of the wreck, thankfully, but after.

My first session, we addressed the sight of the boys lying in the funeral home the first time I saw them afterward. They were perfect, but it still felt like a gut punch every time I thought of it. After less than about ten minutes, I was totally fine with the thought.

We went over a few other things that caused me distress that first go, ending with the guilt I felt for falling in love with another man (more on him in a bit). I had only ever loved Tyler with my whole heart, and I was feeling really guilty for having similar feelings for another person even though Tyler is no longer here. I know I'll always love him, but it wasn't fair to the other man to not get my whole heart. At the end of that part, all I heard was Tyler saying, "It's okay, Jen. I love you." He was talking straight to my soul and releasing me to love again. It left me happy and full of so much more love for Tyler.

My next session, I focused on a few other aspects, one of which was the thought of my guys lying beside our totaled vehicle no longer in their bodies. I was contacted by numerous first responders telling me how they took wonderful care of them, but the idea of my baby boy and love of my life just lying there was too much for me. We addressed it, and at the end, I heard Wyatt say, "We're okay, Momma."

Finally, I brought up sunglasses. A few weeks prior to the wreck, I had taken Wyatt to the ophthalmologist for the first time. His vision was great, but the doc recommended he start wearing sunglasses outside. So Wyatt harped on me for a week to get him sunglasses. Of course, the little two needed them too. I let them each pick a pair from Amazon, and they arrived about a week before the wreck. Wyatt wore his all the time when he went outside; he loved them. When I got the box of stuff back from the jeep, his broken sunglasses were in there along with all the other broken, damaged, and bloodstained possessions of the kids. Since then, my heart would get squeezed every time I saw kids' sunglasses.

We started the session. I went back and forth, allowing my brain to reshuffle the image of his sunglasses and the memories. When I ended, I heard Wyatt say, "We don't need sunglasses here, Momma."

In all cases, it was like they were sitting right beside me talking to me. I told my therapist that exact thing; she loved it. I can now think of all these thoughts, along with a few others, and I am filled with peace. It's all good. I am grateful for this technique and the fact that it literally felt like it was dealing my brain a new deck of cards to operate off. It's a miracle I can think of my boys in all the bad and still have a soul full of love, happiness, and peace, and have the ability to move forward, live my life, and love again.

My Surrender

I wish I could say this came like it would in a movie—me hunched over in a ball, crying my eyes out and praying. But that's just not me, and that's not how I roll with God. I admit, I did have some of those moments, but surrender didn't just wash over me in one fell swoop. Instead, it came in bits and pieces. I know God was up there rolling his eyes, saying, "Come on, Jenni, just give it all to me already." But I'm stubborn and independent, and it took a lot of lessons and canceled plans before I begged him to take the reins.

In the hospital, there wasn't much I could do besides argue with the doctors and tell them they were wrong about every prognosis. Once we got home, I started planning and plotting how to get my boy going. We had in-home therapy, then outpatient. I took him to every type of treatment I could track down in the state.

I got him lined up to go to a hospital in Phoenix. Fell through.

I got him lined up to go to a therapy clinic in Chicago. Fell through.

I got him lined up to go to an amazing clinic in Baltimore. Fell through.

I stumbled upon an inpatient therapy clinic in Spokane. Fell through.

Then God offered up outpatient therapy in Spokane. I was a little disappointed it wouldn't be as intense as inpatient, but I was also very grateful we wouldn't be stuck in a hospital for two months.

The therapists got him in there as often as they could and worked so hard with him. I have to say that kid wins friends everywhere he goes; he's like a little politician—the good kind (wink).

The best part of it all was the time I got to heal. Up to that point, I had been going ninety miles per hour and living solely for my kids. I had zero time for myself to grieve and allow my soul to gather itself. This opportunity gave Weston the therapy he needed, time with his beloved Nana, and me the time to escape outside to think, pray, and move.

I moved through a lot of stuff during those months in Spokane (I don't think it's a coincidence that that's where Tyler grew up). I had good days, but I also had a lot of dark days, a lot of crying, a lot of asking God why and what I was supposed to do now. Like I said, I went through a lot. All the things I needed to work through in order to come out the other side stronger and full of the light he kept me here to spread.

I surrendered Weston's healing to God. Wakely's healing to God. My life to God. I told him he was stuck with us, and we were all his.

I also gave over my hope of another love to him. I had already been praying for a very specific man all year. I had a list. A couple of lists. I knew what I needed, what I wanted, and what this guy had to bring to the table, including loving Jesus and accepting the boys as forever a part of our lives. And that he would have to literally come to my door, because I was inept at dating and had no idea how to meet anyone. I met several amazing guys over the course of the year and wound up with my heart broken because it was me attempting to force and not allowing God to take care of things.

I hit my last straw in Spokane after one more disappointment, and I told God I was done with men; I didn't even want to try anymore.

Shortly after this declaration, I was hiking by myself looking for shed antlers, and it hit me like a train. I was truly happy again. I laughed out loud. I didn't think I would ever be full of joy again, but here I was. I realized life is good, no matter what comes our way. God always has an amazing plan for our lives. We just have to trust, have faith, and live the life he has planned for us.

Because God does indeed have a sense of humor, there's more to this part. A few weeks after my realization and fully understanding I didn't *need* anyone else, this guy friended me on Facebook. He was a friend of my sister-in-law and asked if I needed help with anything around the place. I assured him that I had a lot of projects that needed done. He had been going through a difficult time in his own life and had spent several days fasting and praying, asking God to show him what to do. After one of these prayer sessions, he was on Facebook, and I popped up as a suggested friend. He went with it.

We talked for a couple of weeks and then met for breakfast when he got off shift. He came up to the house after so I could show him what I was thinking, and we said our goodbyes. We hung out a couple of days later, and that's all it took. I quickly realized he was the guy I had been praying for.

I had given God a very specific list of what I would prefer in a potential second husband as Tyler had set the bar very high. Justin marked off every single item, plus many more. Add that to the fact that God literally brought him to my front door. Finding another love as great as what Tyler and I had is a major miracle in my book. Something I never thought I would find again, yet here he is. God is good, especially when you hand over the reins and allow him to do his thing.

Baby Steps

(Contributed by Jen and her family)

March 28, 2021

Wakely woke up on her own. They sedated her again to ensure she didn't hurt herself, but the nurses said she looked around and was fully engaged with her surroundings.

Weston is responding to the corneal exam, and his foot jerks when you run a finger up it.

March 29, 2021

Wakely had an awesome night! This morning she's been responsive to commands. She will hold up two fingers, wiggle her toes on the foot they ask her to, and gives us a weak thumbs-up on both hands! The neurosurgeon is very happy with this so they are removing the Frankenstein bolt from her head right now! They are weaning her off all sedatives. They want to start her on feeds and get some nutrition in her and do some X-rays later today. Big, big steps for this little fighter!

Wes-Man had a solid night, but early this morning his ICP numbers went higher than they liked. This is concerning but also expected, given the severity of his head trauma. They are going to try some different medication, upping his blood pressure, lowering his temperature, and starting him on feeds as well to see if this will drop his numbers. They are also going to try a heavier sedation. The doctor explained that the next twenty-four to forty-eight hours are critical for Wes. We need him to coast through with no major setbacks and no more head surgeries. Please pray that his little body will accept these proposed changes and his ICP numbers drop back down. We want things to stay uneventful for him, for now.

March 30, 2021

They took Miss Wakes off sedation last night at six; she's remained off since then. They extubated her around eight thirty this morning, and she did well with that. She's breathing 100 percent on her own now! They also started feeds for her so she can get some good nutrition going. Wakely has sat up on her own, she's opened her eyes, and she responds to commands but not consistently so, yet. This is completely normal and to be expected with head trauma. She was crying some (it felt so good to hear her little voice, even in that manner), and they've since given her a little extra pain medication to keep her comfortable. She's all snuggled in now for a nap.

Wes had an okay night. His ICP numbers hovered around 24 to 25 all night, but they never went higher, which was a blessing because we found out after the fact that the neurosurgeons were ready to pounce if he hit 26 for any length of time. A change of meds has dropped his numbers, and he's now at 16, so that's a huge win. We're slowly easing out of the critical situation with the swelling. There's a good possibility they'll remove the monitor bolt they placed in his head tomorrow.

He's been heavily sedated since yesterday. He's still completely dependent on the ventilator and that's okay, but his lungs aren't filling up all the way to the bottom, which is causing the bottom part to collapse. They can try some vibration stimulation for this to get him to take deep breaths and reinflate those lungs; the major concern here is for pneumonia. They plan to start feeds on Wes today and get some good nutrition for him as well.

At this time, he's not responding to reflexive tests, but this is not concerning, given his level of sedation. Please keep sending positive vibes that his ICP number stays stable and continues to drop. The doctor did say that he's doing everything she could expect from him at this time so that is a good thing.

They took Jen off sedation at 2:00 p.m. yesterday. They gave her light sedation through the night so she could rest and weaned her off again this morning. The surgeon who performed on her partially torn aorta okayed tube removal because she was able to breath on her own without ventilation. Last I heard, they were going to try to extubate after lunch. Please pray that she does well with this because it will be a big step forward for her. Her lung CT looked good, her ribs will take time to heal, and the doc said her liver laceration should be an easy fix. Our stepdad Rob said she squeezed his hand and looked at him this morning, and she's answering most commands and responding well to reflexive testing!

Jen did great today! They took off her ventilator, and she is breathing great on her own. They lifted sedation enough to have her interact with us, and she passed all her major tests to move forward with extubation. She would look at us, squeeze our hands, and even nod her head when asked questions! However, when they decided to go for the extubation and deflated the cuff around the tube, Jen's airway didn't stay open enough on its own for the doctor to feel comfortable enough removing the breathing tube.

They think she still has some swelling that could make it hard for her to breathe, so we are giving her just a little more time for the swelling to go down and will hopefully try again tomorrow. Even though it's a little set back, all in all the doctors are very pleased with how she is progressing and have high hopes for tomorrow. Thank you all for all the prayers and support!

March 31, 2021

Jen had a great night, and plans for removing her breathing tube were moving forward this morning, but there was still enough swelling in her airway that set us back one more day. The doctors prescribed a steroid to help with inflammation, and we will try again tomorrow. No worries, better to be safe and do it right, and Jen is very much ready to have the tube out.

She is still doing great with everything else (she even waved at me today), just ticked about having a tube down her throat. The

45

doctors and staff have been amazing here, and we couldn't be more thankful that Jen is getting the kind of top-notch care here at Benefis. We are truly blessed for everything and everyone who has been involved with Jen's care here.

April 1, 2021

Wes-Bear is doing so well! Yesterday morning, his ICP numbers dropped to a respectable 12–15 range. This made the neuro team confident enough to remove his Frankenstein bolt, which monitored swelling and oxygen numbers. This means they are no longer worried about swelling for Wes. He's made it past the peak swelling time! This is awesome!

Our guy is now coughing spontaneously and trying to open his left eye. They've started weaning him off the more severe sedative, and he's responding to reflexive testing. They removed his chest tubes yesterday, and he did great with that. He's also breathing over the ventilator some, and last night he reached for and placed his hand on the ventilator, which they are happy with because it means his brain is giving him commands and telling him, *there's something going on out there and we're not sure we like it.* Purposeful movement!

Vibration stimulation is also helping him draw those much-needed deep breaths so his lungs can reinflate fully and cough up some of the gunk in there. He's also waking up to light touch… movement!

He'll get an MRI today, and they plan to remove his central line. They want to remove the catheter tomorrow, and they'll be watching his lungs closely and plan for extubation when they think he's ready for it.

All this is really good news for Weston! Our guy is almost out of the woods! He was a bit too shy for a pic, and to be honest…he looks pretty gruesome with all of his stitches and swelling. But we know our sweet boy is in there, and we'll share a pic when we feel it's appropriate.

Meet the "Dragon Princess," aptly named by the head of pediatrics at Harborview Medical. Wakely is doing fantastic! After the central line and catheter removal (which she did well with), we had a rough morning yesterday, lots of crying and frustration for her. The neuro team had a look and did some tests and seemed quite disappointed as they left. This hurt! Come to find out, Miss Wakes had a point to make...she is no show pony, and she is not here to perform for anybody!

After a good, healthy, much-needed BM, Wako's day improved by the minute! She went from zero tracking with her eyes, very little response to commands, and an overall lack of communication...to following and tracking different voices, focusing in on some new unicorn posters sent by her classmates, giving knucks (followed by a shooting gun), thumbs-up, and reaching out for a familiar hand for comfort. She would even get close to giving us her little trademark smirk when we'd chant at her... All of this is extraordinary, given the nature of her trauma.

But the best thing, the thing that made me cry with joy, is the way we ended our day. Wakes and I said our prayers. I led the way because our sweet girl hasn't said a word yet, and when we got to the end, I said, "Amen." Then I looked at our sweet girl...and our feisty, ferocious, majestical girl said the most beautiful word I've ever heard in my life... "Amen!" I truly believe that this is a direct result of the outpouring of love and prayers that have been said for our Wako. Thank you, Lord, and thank you, prayer warriors, for your ceaseless faith!

PS. The nurses that work with her refer to her as their spicy little peanut.

April 3, 2021

Jen has been extubated and can write, walk a few steps, talk, and function. Hallelujah! She is the toughest woman I have ever known, and her will is incomparable. Please pray that she finds comfort and peace as she digests the unfathomable. We also request that you give her and her caregivers space as they navigate through this.

Our Wakely is doing very well. She is getting very good at communicating her needs. She still isn't speaking, but she mouths words we ask her to repeat. She can sit up and stand briefly, and we're working on taking a step. She beats us at thumb wars and counts to five on her fingers, and her swallow reflex looks good. We're hoping to try some soft foods soon. We've been told if she continues to progress in the next two weeks, she will be transferred to the Children's Hospital about four miles away to undergo what is essentially a therapy boot camp, where they work with her on basic functions. She is a fighter, and I know she will continue to improve daily!

And now our Wes-Bear. Unfortunately, two nights ago, Weston took a big step backward. His scans came back to show that a small injury to the inside of his carotid artery was sending miniscule clots up to his brain. The clots caused Wes to undergo multiple strokes, and the doctors were unable to see them. This caused significant damage to our guy's already damaged brain.

They had to put the bolt back in so they could monitor his ICPs and assess his swelling accordingly. They got that part under control and took the bolt back out yesterday. He is very sedated and comfortable.

The doctors don't consider him stable, but he is more so today than he was yesterday. This is a major blow for us because they explained the damage to his brain is quite severe—estimating that the only part of his brain not damaged is about the size of a walnut.

If everything continues forward with no more setbacks, they said he will be in the ICU for at least three to four more weeks before they feel confident in making a new plan for him. Our hearts are heavy, and we pray that someday we can understand this path that we've set out on. Thank you all for your continued prayers and support in this very dark time for us.

April 11, 2021

I just wanted to let all of you wonderful souls know that Mom and I made it to Seattle this morning. It was amazing getting to see my babies finally. Wakes is doing awesome, just about ready to start rehab and therapy. Weston is breathing some on his own, but he still needs all your prayers for a strong body and mind. I know the Lord has plans for us so I'm not scared, but I also know he needs all the help he can get, so please spend time every day this week praying for Weston. Thank you.

April 12, 2021

I was able to spend most of my morning with Wes-Bear today. The good news is he's still in there; the bad news is his body and brain took a lot from the wreck.

Due to sedation, they're not entirely sure what we have to work with. Thanks to that, they're slowly backing his sedation off while still keeping him comfortable so that one day soon we'll have a better idea about our Wes-Man.

Until then, I ask that you pray for healing and strength over his body and mind. I ask that you pray for the miracle I'm so desperately pleading for. I ask that you pray that his little body is strongly knit back together, including the broken bones he suffered in the wreck.

Thank you, heavenly Father, for giving me the chance to see my babies again.

April 13, 2021

Not a lot of changes today.

Wakely has been busy with therapy and is doing amazing (she's currently enjoying her afternoon nap).

Wes-Man is still deep in thought, and, I'm praying, healing from the inside out.

We were just told yesterday that they're going to try and move Wes to the Children's Hospital when they move Wakely for rehab. He will not be going for rehab but rather to continue his recovery in the ICU.

We are still not sure what the future holds for him, but deep down in my heart, my God and my faith tell me Wes will be okay. Because of that, I believe and know that one day soon I will look into his beautiful blue eyes and see a gleam of mischief.

Please continue to pray.

Thank you, each and every one of you, for your prayers, thoughts, and gifts that you have sent.

We are truly a blessed family.

April 16, 2021

Today was a good day for us—both kids are now at the Children's Hospital and getting amazing care!

We have a plan to get Wes moving in the right direction, and Wakes is going to hit therapy hard tomorrow.

It's pretty over here in Seattle, but I'm missing MT like crazy—we're ready for that miracle any day!

April 18, 2021

I hope everyone took this Sunday for a day of rest.

We're continuing to pray for our Weston, knowing and trusting that God is healing him from the inside out.

Today Weston's soccer team (the Weir Warriors) played and won their first game! He's going to be so excited when I tell him.

Wakes also had a big day—after she worked hard all day yesterday to prove she could drink as much as she needed to, they agreed to take her tube out. They followed through, and now our beautiful girl has much more freedom to move, talk, and smile.

Thank you all. For everything.

April 20, 2021

I'm asking all our friends, family, and followers to say a prayer over Jen. I know we're all in awe that this amazing, tough, tenacious woman has fought and scratched her way out of her hospital bed and put her pain and suffering on the back burner so she could go to Seattle and be there for her babies. But now a lot of the realities and grief have begun to set in.

Doctors have told Jen that they're not happy with Weston's progress. That they "highly expect him to have severe deficits if he comes out of this." No mother is ever prepared to hear these words about her child, let alone a mother who is trying to cope with the loss of her husband and son.

Jen is missing Tyler, her best friend, partner, and soul mate… the one she would talk to in this very hard time to bounce ideas and thoughts off. Our mom is there, and so is Tyler's, but we all know it's not the same as having your spouse there for support and comfort.

Jen's doing her very best, but she's struggling. I asked if she would mind if I share this with you all and ask that you pray over her heart and mind as she continues to fight for Weston. Jen is a woman of enduring faith, but she's asking you to pray with her, and pray for her now, as her faith is being tested like never before.

Thank you all.

April 23, 2021

Me again. Just had a little news to share.

First off, the sassy pants was discharged today! She's back at the Ronald McDonald House with us and her "jailbreak" cake.

She's headed back to MT to begin outpatient therapy in Great Falls, and she's stoked to get home!

The meeting for Weston last night went very well. Thankfully I had settled down from Tuesday (after a good-intentioned doctor decided I needed to really hear Weston's prognosis—he would be severely handicapped and have intense deficits in everything his entire life).

All the doctors were very open to chatting with us, and the head MD finally said what I've been waiting for: "Weston really just needs time to heal."

Yes. Yes. Yes.

They're keeping him as comfortable as possible, but ultimately it comes down to the miracle I know is coming.

Please continue to pray.

Specifically, please pray for:

- healing and restoration of Weston's brain (it is swollen and angry right now)
- that Wes's brain will begin doing what it needs to do for maintenance
- the neurology team had a successful surgery to drain the cerebral spinal fluid off his brain so that it can actually work the way it's supposed to
- healing for Weston's body

Again, I know in my soul that God is working on Wes right now. I know that he has plans for my boy.

Thank you all for your prayers and support.

April 26, 2021

Hey, friends, we need some strong prayers tonight. Weston is headed into the OR for an abdominal surgery. They're hoping to figure out what's been causing him so much trouble and repair it so that his little body can heal.

Prayers for Weston and his surgeons, please.

April 27, 2021

Good morning and thank you all for your prayers!

Weston went in for surgery late last night. It was basically an exploratory surgery. They knew something was wrong but were unable to figure out what based on the X-rays and scans.

They went in assuming to find large perforations and/or necrosis in his intestines. They told me they would have to remove whatever they could to get his guts moving and working again, leaving him fully reliant on a tube for nutrition.

Terrified, I asked them to please take care of my baby.

They called back in the middle of the night after surgery. It went well.

They didn't find what they thought. Actually, his intestines looked really healthy. What they did find was a spot on his bowel where there was some scar tissue that had caused the bowel to turn inside out on itself—blocking everything from coming out.

They fixed that, sewed him up, and now my boy is back on the road to healing. I pray his little body doesn't have to deal with any more stressors, just healing.

Thank you all again, and please keep praying for my boy.

May 2, 2021

A lot of people have been asking for updates on Miss Wakely, our Dragon Warrior Princess.

We've come to realize that we let everyone know that Seattle Children's discharged her early (one week of therapy instead of the originally planned three). But everyone wants to know how this little lady is doing.

Well, we're thrilled to share that Wakes is all there! Cognitively and physically, her functions are amazing! There are a few small hiccups… Sometimes she can't find the word she's looking for, but her therapist assured us her words are there; it just takes a bit more work for her to find a specific word from time to time.

Once in a while, her short-term memory fails her, and we have found that some details in the weeks prior to the accident have slipped her mind. Thankfully, she remembers nothing of the actual accident. In addition, when our girl gets tired, her left hand and leg get weak (damage to the right hemisphere of the brain affects the left side of your body). Her therapists have assured us that this is all completely normal, and they're confident all these small things will improve with time.

There are still some unknowns on long-term outlook. Wakes may have trouble as an adult with organizational skills and decision-making (ummm…don't we all?), but these are very minor concerns, given the extraordinary obstacles this little girl has overcome.

Wakes is back in MT; she's in Meemaw Becky's care for the time being. They're talking about sending her back to school part-time to see how she handles it. And she's super pumped for her kinder graduation at OLL next month! She will also have to continue with some outpatient therapy at home in Great Falls.

In short, Wakely is a walking, talking miracle, and we are so blessed and grateful for every single prayer that was sent up on her behalf. Her sassy spirit and determination are an inspiration, and I can't wait to see what the future holds for this beautiful little WARRIOR!

We ask for continued prayers for Weston as he continues his battle. We know miracles happen, and we know we have the very best prayer warriors on our side.

Again, thank you all for the continued and unwavering support and kindness. We feel your love…we really do.

May 2, 2021

Update from Seattle.

This week was a long week for Wes.

He had abdominal surgery late Monday night, which, thank God, turned out to be successful and none of the bad stuff they expected to find turned up.

Wednesday brought a second call from the surgeon (I was back in GF to see the doc myself and get funeral stuff done). This time they wanted to take him back to the OR to get a drain in his head and the pressure out. That surgery also went well, and his head looks so much better.

Two surgeries have left the little guy in a ton of pain, but they're doing a fantastic job managing it.

Now he's relaxed, able to rest and HEAL!

Wakes has been wearing her Meemaw out and eating all the ice cream she can get her hands on. She's doing amazing and will be starting some rehab next week.

As for the funerals for my guys, I'm planning on a vigil the night of May 21 and a funeral mass on May 22—both will be held at Our Lady of Lourdes Parish in GF.

Lastly, I want to say a huge thank-you to you all. Without your prayers and support, I don't think we'd have made it this far.

As for the generosity of my hometown, the Great Falls community, friends, and strangers from in and out of state, I am completely overwhelmed and humbled. Thank you does not come close to expressing what's in my heart, but it's all I can say. Thank you and God bless you all.

May 4, 2021

More prayers for Wes! He's doing great; we're just heading toward a big step, hopefully forward. The docs would like to try and get the breathing tube out of his throat. God willing, he'll be successful at breathing on his own without support. Otherwise, we'll be looking at a tracheostomy to keep his lungs moving.

May 6, 2021

Wes has been off the ventilator since one today and is breathing on his own! Please continue to pray for his little body to stay strong.

May 7, 2021

Weston is still going strong this morning. No intervention throughout the night—just him and his strong little body fighting hard.

Jessi posting here: It's National Nurses Week. Throughout this entire ordeal, we have encountered the most extraordinary nurses, from Benefis, to Harborview, to Seattle Children's. We have had nurses cry with us, laugh with us, and make us feel not so alone.

My third night in Seattle, Wakely was having a very rough night. A nurse called our hotel and asked if I would like to come and try to comfort her. Of course I did, but it was one in the morning. I asked how was the best way to get there this time of night, Uber? Taxi? She says, what hotel are you at? I told her, and she says, I'll be there to pick you up in ten minutes.

Another nurse had shared our story with her mother-in-law. The next day, the mother-in-law and the nurse's little daughter had sent homemade lasagna for us so we wouldn't get burned out on hospital food and takeout. Homemade lasagna never tasted so good!

We came in one morning to find that Wes had to change rooms after a very busy night in the ICU. We walked into his new room to find that the night nurse had taken down and rehung the *hundreds* of "get well" cards, prayer chains, etc., that had been hanging in his old room. This was the same nurse who apologized over and over again the night they found Wes's stroke. It wasn't his fault, but he felt so very bad about the whole situation.

Nurses have been there to break down the medical jargon after rounds every morning and put it in layman terms for us to understand. We've had nurses go to battle for us and with us when at times we felt like the doctors weren't on the same page with our goals. And I know Jen had a couple of nurses go to battle for her while she was at Benefis.

To sum it up, I just want to say thank you to these amazing people who have made this incredibly terrible time just a little bit more bearable. These folks have the biggest hearts, and I know those hearts take a beating when they become so invested in their patients. It's a thankless job, but we appreciate you and are in awe of your skill, resolve, and compassion. To you and all nurses, we send out our love and respect! Thank you!

The little munchkin got to go give school a whirl for a bit this morning. I'm guessing it went well!

May 18, 2021

Big news for Weston: after seven weeks, he's finally getting booted out of ICU!

Now we're off to another section of the hospital with, hopefully, more rehab worked into his day.

His surgery yesterday went well. The surgery team saw no sign of infection and were able to get his scalp pulled back together. Sunday he's headed back into surgery for an internal shunt (the external one he has now is a much higher risk for infection) and then he gets a break for a few weeks until he'll finally get his bone put back in!

Our Wes-Man is doing awesome, being a strong little dude every day. Please continue to pray for him, thank you!

May 23, 2021

Thank you to each and every one of you for all you have done for my family. The support has been beyond anything I ever could've imagined.

My family and Tyler's family have been such a rock for me, and I am forever grateful.

Please keep the prayers coming, they're more powerful than we know.

Thank you.

May 27, 2021

 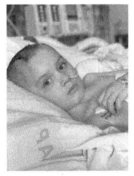 

Okay, it's time for a real-life Weston update. I have been going back and forth about sharing these, but I've had an overwhelming urge to let you all know that the POWER OF PRAYER IS REAL.

The first picture is the first time I saw Weston after the wreck in the first week of April. Our boy was in very rough shape.

He had five broken bones, multiple rib fractures, blood on his lungs, a ruptured spleen, and a severe traumatic brain injury. Probably some stuff I'm missing.

The picture of him looking at the camera was from last week and taken by amazing friends who volunteered to go stay with him while we all came home for the funeral.

The last one of him in the helmet was taken Tuesday by my mother-in-law, who flew straight back to Seattle after the funeral.

That's right, on Tuesday my boy sat on the edge of his bed! The first time he has not been lying flat on his back in the last almost nine weeks.

I've had so many people ask me how Weston is, and when I tell them he's improving every single day, they look at me like I'm a crazy person who's lost her grip with reality.

But I need every one of you to know that my beautiful boy is a miracle who is only beginning to show us what he's capable of. Weston is going to move mountains, of that I am certain.

So what I need to say is:

Prayer is powerful.

God is good.

My baby is healing every day.

Please keep praying, y'all are doing more for us then you can possibly imagine.

May 28, 2021

Wakely and Momma update.

First off, today Wakely graduated kindergarten 🐾. I hoped she'd be able to attend with her classmates, and she did! God is good.

Second, the three of us that survived the wreck are very blessed to be here today. Ultimately, none of us should have made it that day.

It just so happened there were multiple doctors immediately on the scene as well as Belt Fire and EMS to get us to the hospital.

Wakely suffered a TBI and a broken clavicle and had very unstable breathing for a long time. Yet our little warrior is here today. Crackin' jokes and loving life. She has months of OT and speech ahead of her, but she's here.

I also had a TBI, but didn't have to have my skull split open like the kids. My liver was lacerated, both lungs were collapsed, fourteen fractures dotted my ribs, and two of the three layers of my aorta were torn (which is why I now have a stent).

I'm mostly healed, still have a few sore ribs and still working on getting my strength back and having a heart rate that isn't through the ceiling all the time.

All in all, prayers work, and we are both hanging in there.

PS. Weston spent forty-five minutes in a wheelchair today.

God is good. Please continue to pray. Miracles are real and happening all around us.

June 2, 2021

Back in Seattle with Weston, and the little dude is hanging tough. Sounds like the skull plate is going back in about two weeks.

Please continue to pray with us.

The Most Powerful Healing Prayer by St. Padre Pio

Heavenly Father, I thank you for loving Weston.

I thank you for sending your Son, Our Lord Jesus Christ, to the world to save and to set Weston free.

I trust in your power and grace that sustain and restore Weston.

Loving Father, touch Wes now with your healing hands, for I believe that your will is for Weston to be well in mind, body, soul, and spirit.

Cover Wes with the most precious blood of your Son, our Lord Jesus Christ, from the top of his head to the soles of his feet.

Cast anything that should not be in him.

Root out any unhealthy and abnormal cells.

Open any blocked arteries or veins and rebuild and replenish any damaged areas.

Remove all inflammation and cleanse any infection by the power of Jesus's precious blood.

Let the fire of your healing love pass through Weston's entire body to heal and make new any diseased areas so that his body will function the way you created it to function.

Touch also his mind and his emotion, even the deepest recesses of his heart.

Saturate his entire being with your presence, love, joy, and peace, and draw him ever closer to you every moment of his life.

And Father, fill Weston with your Holy Spirit, and empower him to do your works so that his life will bring glory and honor to your holy name.

I ask this in the name of our Lord Jesus Christ. Amen.

June 9, 2021

Weston continues to keep fighting.

He went in for surgery at noon. They told me it would be three to four hours, and then he'd be headed back to the PICU.

An hour and a half later, they called to say he was out! The surgeons said it went very well; he's headed to recovery and then gets to go back to his regular room, not PICU.

Baby steps. Baby steps every single day.

Keep fighting, Weston.

Please continue to pray for fusion of the bone and mending of his brain.

God is good.

June 15, 2021

Hey, guys! So a quick update on Wes-Man.

He's been doing phenomenal since his surgery last week—his little body was just waiting to get put back together.

He's been outside every day for the last four days and is lovin' getting some of that beautiful sunshine.

We're still working on getting the shunt setting just right; they're doing a scan tomorrow to take a peek at his fluid levels.

Tomorrow is also the big day for his next surgery. He's getting a G-tube put in (a feeding tube through the skin into his stomach— goodbye, tube through the nose!) and then on to rehab!

He's getting stronger and doing different tasks every day.

Please keep the little dude in your prayers.

God is good.

June 22, 2021

It's been a bit, so I figured I better give a Wes update.

Our little bear is working his tail off in rehab. He has physical therapy, occupational therapy, and speech therapy twice a day now.

I came home on Thursday last week, and on Friday his Nana sent me the best video I've ever seen…she had my boy GIGGLING! She was giving him kisses and teasing him, and he was a giggling little fool. Literally the best noise I've ever heard.

When Jessi was in Seattle a couple of weekends ago, she had him doing "knucks" and blowing it up and having thumb wars. When we asked him where his nose, eyes, mouth, and ear were, he touched each one respectively.

Slowly but surely, God is working in my boy. The road is long, but Wes keeps pushing forward.

He is the strongest person I know, and he will do great things with his life.

Please keep the prayers coming.

God is good.

June 28, 2021

Update on the Weir front. Biggest news: Weston has a tentative discharge in the next couple of weeks! Now the real work begins at home.

Momma Jen and Wakes made a trip to Glacier for the half marathon—Jen and Tyler had been signed up for a year, so she decided to give it a go. Made it across the finish line and got to spend some good time in God's country.

God is good.

July 10, 2021

Hey, guys, just a quick update! Weston is supposed to be headed home this coming week, woohoo!

However, his calcium levels have been high. This could cause a delay in discharge. His levels have been steadily decreasing, but they're still a little higher than the docs like.

They contemplated giving him a med for it, but I opted not to do it since it causes flu-like symptoms for several days and is hard on the kidneys.

I'm asking everyone to please pray for his calcium levels to decrease to safe levels naturally so that we can make it home this week and keep this boy on the path of healing. Thank you.

God is good.

July 13, 2021

Well, folks, the stars aligned, the docs gave us their blessing, and God heard your prayers—Weston "The Bear" Weir made it back to MT today.

He is currently chillin' in the living room surrounded by his sister and cousins. The boy is content.

A huge thank-you to all of you, your prayers, your kind words, and your donations. You all have meant a lot to us. We are so happy to be back home!

Wes has a lot of work ahead of him, but we have in-home rehab lined up, and now he gets time to rest and heal.

God. Is. Good.

July 18, 2021

Hey, gang! Wes is loving being at home and has gotten to see a few friendly faces.

While in-home therapy is fantastic, we're hoping for bigger things for Weston. We're working on getting a referral for a therapy center where he can get intensive work and have the best shot at recovery.

What we're saying is, we need more prayers for a miracle for this little eight-year-old boy to get referred and accepted to a center that can give him the therapy he needs to make the recovery I know he's going to make.

Thank you.

God is good.

July 24, 2021

Losing someone you love does not mean they're GONE.

Sure, you can't hug them, kiss them, or yell at them anymore.

But you have to be willing to look for them.

Wyatt always wore a feather in his hat—now, whenever we find a feather (and we've found a lot), we know it's Wyatt telling us he loves us.

Tyler was an exceptional prop mechanic on the C-130s—now every time we see one fly over (which is nearly every day), Wakely says it's her daddy saying, "I love you, baby girl."

They're always around; just open your heart and let them in.

God is good.

July 29, 2021

So, no big deal—actually, a really big deal!—but my boy started giving himself a drink of chocolate milk…it's his life force!

GOD IS GOOD.

July 30, 2021

This little boy had another first today!

We finally got PT out to the house, and she WORKED HIM OVER!

He stood twice for over ten seconds and sat on my exercise ball while we moved him all around.

He only got mad once, and now he's exhausted.

It takes a lot of small steps to climb a mountain.

God is good.

August 1, 2021

The last four months have been hard, to say the least.

We lost Tyler and Wyatt, holes that will never be filled until we see them again.

We suffered physically and emotionally, and Weston still has a big mountain ahead of him.

Yet, I know we'll be okay.

When they finally let me wake up and told me what had happened, I didn't scream and lash out. Instead, I was filled with peace, and faith filled my heart. It's something I can't explain but still feel every day. God is good.

We were not only blessed to survive, but we have been blessed with so much from all of you.

The amazing care we received here in Great Falls from the first responders, doctors, nurses, therapists, and everything Seattle did for the kids. There are truly some amazing people in the medical community.

I'm grateful for my siblings who dropped everything to go and be with the kids in Seattle when I couldn't be; my mother-in-law for staying the duration in Seattle with and without me; and my mom, who has put her entire life on hold to be here with me and the kids.

All the countless people who sent gifts, blankets, cards, and money. Those who have offered help and done jobs around the house. All the prayers that are put forth on our behalf. Friends who are only a text away and often here anyway to visit. I am humbled beyond words at the outpouring of support and love we have and continue to receive.

There are days when I'm so tired I can barely function, but our work has just begun. I don't know why we beat the odds, but we did. God kept us here for a reason, and I intend to fulfill that reason.

I have no idea what his plans are, but I do know I've received so many messages from people I don't know telling me their faith is renewed, that they are going to church again after several years of not going, that, yes, God is good.

I feel like this is only the beginning. It's now our turn to be a blessing to others. The heartbreak sucks, but it's something I will deal with to help more people know Jesus better.

Thank you all so very much.

God is good.

August 21, 2021

Hey! It's been a few days, so I thought I'd check in.

On the Wes front, the kid is a little badass. He's wheeling himself in circles in his chair with his right arm, he stood for a full two minutes at PT on Monday, he's been laughing hysterically when his sister sings her made-up diarrhea song. He and I did a little grappling on the bed the other day; he pretended to cry when I got him. He's working hard every chance he gets. He'll be flipping tables at rehab.

As of right now, we have a telehealth eval scheduled with Phoenix on September 8. We have five other referrals out but have heard nothing else.

Wakely will be heading to first grade in about two weeks. Despite her arguments, I think she's ready to get cracking!

Other than that, I just wanted to share these few pics that have been popping up in my FB memories every morning to take a little nibble out of my heart.

God, our lives were so good. Remember that every day. Don't get hung up on the stupid shit, or fight about things that don't really matter. Be grateful for every day you have with those you love. You honestly have no idea what your life has in store for you.

I didn't even kiss Tyler that morning because we were rushing around trying to get the kids out the door to go skiing.

Kiss, love, hold, thank, and appreciate today and every day that you can.

Life is crazy, but God is good.

August 22, 2021

Momma Jen here. I had the privilege of spending the last week in DC on behalf of Tyler and his incredible accomplishment. I went there thinking it was for his regional award. It wasn't until I arrived that I found out it was for the national award—Air National Guard Outstanding NCO of the Year—of course, he went all the way.

The trip itself was amazing; the ANG went above and beyond for us. The other three awardees were the best! I assumed I would be the odd man out, but no. They took me right in and are some of the most phenomenal individuals I've ever met.

The entire time I thought how much Tyler would've loved the entire experience, and I would give anything for him to have been there to accept what he had worked so hard for.

I hope you all are grateful every day for what our service members do for our great nation.

September 6, 2021

Happy Labor Day, everyone!

Just wanted to do a quick Wes update. Bottom line, the boy is amazing. He's doing new tasks every day.

He's brushing his teeth, wipes his mouth after each bite with a napkin, makes a purposeful noise repeatedly for his ST, bats a balloon around that's tied under the stairs, eats most meals by mouth, has a mean right jab, and waved goodbye to his ST the other day—I almost bawled.

The most exciting thing, as far as I'm concerned, is that today he smiled with both sides of his face! Why is this a big deal? Because since the wreck he has been neglecting his left side.

When he smiles or makes any facial expression, it's always just the right side. Today after I smooched his cheek, he was grinning with his whole face. It's the most beautiful thing I've ever seen! His left side is waking up.

Eval with Phoenix on Wednesday!

God is good.

September 8, 2021

Thought I'd give an update for the big day.

This morning we had a telehealth eval with Phoenix. I was so excited and anxious for it.

Unfortunately, it did not go as planned. The neurologist we spoke with didn't even know what our goals were—to get him into the inpatient rehab. After I told him that, he kept referring us to other facilities.

The ST and PT were here so they could help answer any questions. We were all baffled by the end of the conversation. I don't know if someone dropped the ball or if communication down there is just not what I expected, but wow.

HOWEVER, an angel of a friend had recently been in contact with a therapist friend of hers. She had recommended a place in Minneapolis and another in Chicago and had already been in contact with both places.

Everything was faxed to both facilities today thanks to our outstanding ST.

I'm bummed things didn't go as planned this morning, but God will put us exactly where we're supposed to be.

Finally, last night when I was getting ready to take Wes into his room for bed, I told him to say, "Night, Wakes." As I spun him around, he SAID, "Ni, Way"! His first spoken words since the wreck. Of course, he wouldn't do it again, but…

GOD IS GOOD.

September 9, 2021

I'm sorry, I'm severely overposting this week, but this boy is blowing my mind!

I bought some veggie straws just for him to try, and he's not only mowing them, he's also feeding himself like a little eight-year-old boy should!

And today, after I gave him a bath, I was drying him off on my bed. He was doing his pretend fuss, and I told him to at least say Mom if he was gonna make noise. He worked for a minute and then yelled, "Maaa!" It was music to my ears, and, of course, I cried.

Chicago called today, and they think with his progress, Wes would be a great fit for them! Still waiting to hear from Minneapolis.

God is good.

September 13, 2021

Hey! So, this weekend I emailed the Kennedy Krieger Institute about our referral. Today they called me, had yet to see a referral, but the gal emailed the forms they needed, and we got our records faxed over.

This place has been top on our list since the beginning, but I wasn't sure what our chances were. The good thing is Weston is now on their radar!

Please send up your prayers tonight that our guy gets a chance here, thank you! And if not here, somewhere else soon.

God is good.

September 16, 2021

Wes news!

The boy is headed to Chicago Shriners! I talked to them yesterday, asked when they could get him in, and they said as soon as I could get him there. It looks like an amazing place!

I talked to Kennedy Krieger today (the one I posted about the other day), and they are several months out so he's on their wait list. If all goes well, we'll spend some time in Chicago, come home for a bit, then head to Baltimore.

Wakely has taken on the role as in-house speech therapist and, so far, has gotten Weston to add *Meemaw, Wes, Wy, Bye, Butt,* and *Wee-Wee* (their favorite) to his vocabulary.

God is good.

September 18, 2021

Wes-Bear has had a chatty morning. Up to this point, he's been saying single words when prompted and with a lot of effort.

When I went in to get him up this morning, I said good morning, and he said it back. Then I told him I loved him, and he said, "Love you."

Then he had breakfast, and Wakes was talking with him. She told him to say *beer*. And he did. I asked him why he said beer! And he said, "Because Wakes told me to."

Then Wakes asked him why he had a big butt, and he said, "Because God made it."

He went on and on talking. Wakes was flinging a toy around and dropped it. She asked where it went, and he said, "It's under the TV."

I had music playing, and he started singing along to "Dirt on My Boots." I sneezed, and he said, "Bless you." I told him, "Deal," and he said, "Deal McNeal." He asked for pizza for lunch and to watch *Robin Hood* this afternoon.

This boy is coming back so fast, and he's still got his sassiness and sense of humor. After a day of talking, he's exhausted, but, oh my, he's amazing.

God is good!

September 24, 2021

Weston paid his classmates a visit today, and they were all thrilled to see him. He may have beaten them all in thumb wars... just happened to be on a beautiful afternoon and snow-cone day at school.

On the rehab front, we will not be heading to Chicago. Their COVID restrictions are off the charts so, for now, we're going to transition to outpatient rehab here (he's maxed out with what he can do at home for PT) and tap into our local resources. We'll let everyone see what MT is capable of. I have a feeling this boy is going to continue to thrive!

Yesterday, we were practicing Wakely's spelling words in the car. She stopped to mull it over, and Wes took over and started spelling the words for her. Today his ST was giving him a word and asking him to put it in a sentence—he came up with some pretty fantastic sentences.

This morning, he told me I don't cook well and he can cook way better cheeseburgers than me.

Amazing doesn't even begin to describe what this boy is. God is good.

October 3, 2021

Sunday update. Weston is doing amazing. Yes, I'm saying that because I'm his momma. But I'm also saying that because I remember vividly what I experienced when I first got over to Seattle.

The boy never should've survived, but he did. They told me I was going to have to make the decision to "pull the plug" or not. They told me that he would be severely damaged and disabled, if he even survived.

I say now what I said then. My God is bigger than us, bigger than medicine, bigger than all doctors no matter their experience or degree.

Weston survived the wreck, and in the last six months, he has already done significantly more than they predicted he would do in his entire life. My God is big; he loves us and has plans for us that most of us cannot even begin to fathom.

Nobody gets to limit us; we only limit ourselves. We (the Weirs) decided long ago to do things our way (which is genuinely stubborn, pigheaded, and never quitting).

When we set goals, those goals become reality, one way or another. This is no different. Weston will do everything he ever wants to do, physically and intellectually. Wakely will do great things and live an amazing life. I will do my part to continue to help others in any capacity possible.

I have been busy getting people and logistics squared away to get Weston the help he needs. We're heading to outpatient therapy here in Great Falls between the two hospitals. We have aquatic therapy lined up with the Peak. We're headed to an amazing doctor in Billings this week and going to Missoula for a treatment from a gal who practices the Feldenkrais method.

I'm also looking into a tutor to help keep Wes up to speed with his education since rehab is our top priority right now. I have been in contact with Baltimore again, praying that pans out after the first of the year.

I'm definitely thinking outside the box here, but I feel like that's oftentimes the best way to go about things.

For specific prayer requests:

- We can get Wes all the help he needs to maximize recovery
- Thanks for his continued and complete recovery
- For Wake's little heart and mind to heal and be at peace; she misses her daddy and brother so much
- Momma Weir needs sleep and continued peace in her heart

Pray often. It's a powerful weapon.
God is good.

October 10, 2021

Weston update for the last week.

First of all, look at this picture. You see that left leg crossed over the right? He could not even handle lifting his leg before; now it's relaxed…and moving a little bit!!

Okay, let me start at the beginning. Monday, we made a trip to Billings to see Dr. Fike, an amazing chiropractor. He adjusted a few places on Wes with his adjuster gun and then recommended some natural supplements to give Wes's little body a boost and allow his brain to heal (Momma got some too).

Then he had outpatient OT twice; both times he did amazing! Sat on an exercise ball like a champ.

We met with a trainer at the Peak, and he'll begin aquatic therapy this week—he is super stoked to get in the pool!

Lastly, we drove to Missoula on Friday and met with an amazing woman who practices the Feldenkrais method (Google it; it's fascinating). She works with the brain and body to essentially retrain the brain to do what it needs to do. It's because of her work and what she had me do with him at home that his leg is so mobile and flexible right now.

Oh, final tidbit—I had an early Friday morning call with Baltimore and they're ready to take him for their day therapy program! We could've left in November but then would've been gone for the holidays, and I think it's best to be together with Wakes then, so we'll leave after the first of the year for four to six weeks!

I'm excited to keep working on everything here until we head east.

Hope you all had a fabulous weekend!

God is good!

October 17, 2021

I saw this the other day and it stopped me in my tracks. Tyler was our King Lion (self-proclaimed, but we all went with it).

He was the smartest, strongest person I've ever known. He was funny, a huge asshole, and always said what he thought—like it or not.

He was in constant search of knowledge and always pushing himself trying to find that best version of him—he'd go on long runs with a mouth full of water and hold it there until he finished. I tried it once and only made it a hundred yards.

When I came to after the wreck, I asked why Tyler didn't help us. Because even if he had to crawl or drag himself, he would've done whatever he could to save his family. Finally, they told me his neck was broken on impact. That finally made sense to me; only death could stop him.

He never took the easy way out. He joined the AF with a contract for pararescue, then had his dreams shattered when he was medically pulled because of pneumonia from the drownproofing. He then moved on to SERE but was so weak from the pneumonia still that he couldn't get through the last test. Finally, he found his niche as an engine mechanic, and he was one of the best fucking mechanics the AF had. He was still working toward another chance at SERE when the wreck happened.

He had given thirteen years to the AF, four years to SAR, and three years to ski patrol—all of which he loved and felt called to do.

The man was never satisfied. And, while he had yet to reach his full God-given potential at the age of thirty-five, he was damn close. Part of me is grateful that he got to go out as the savage King Lion he was and never had to go through old age and the eventual breakdown of the body.

We both agreed long ago that age was only a number and an excuse to stop living. So, in King Lion spirit, I'm carrying on for him and am going to live every part of that epic life we talked about for all those years.

Don't waste a single day or take any moment for granted. Life is precious.

Until we meet again, stay strong and savage, King Lion.

October 28, 2021

Good morning!

The kids are doing great, excited for Halloween. Wakes is going to use her same costume from last year (first time ever), a sword horse (unicorn), and Weston wanted to be a knight in shining armor—I told him that was a perfect costume!

The little boy is still crushing it. He's had two aquatic therapy sessions with an amazing trainer from the Peak, which he absolutely loves. We went to Kalispell last week to have a new G-tube put in.

We have yet to use it, but it's so nice not to have the long tube dragging around.

We were going to wait to go to Baltimore until after the first of the year, but I just asked if we could go sooner. He's getting outpatient here, but I think it would be beneficial to get him intense therapy now rather than wait. We may just have to have a belated Christmas celebration.

Prayers for Weston that he can find the mental and physical strength to do what he needs to do to get out of that chair.

Prayers for Wakely's heart, mind, and soul that she can continue to carry on and be happy.

Prayers for Momma to have the strength, endurance, and fortitude to keep fighting the good fight and be the best she can be for herself and her kids.

Thank you.

God is good.

November 5, 2021

You know how I've always said that God has us?

Well, one week before the wreck, we were at my sister's house for a big cousin birthday. She had just gotten a new pup, and, of course, I fell in love.

She mentioned that the gal had one left. Tyler told me absolutely not. I said we could "just look."

The gal brought over this fuzzy little black ball of fur. He walked over and lay down on Tyler's feet. He looked at me with a big ol' grin and said, I think we might need him.

I couldn't believe it! I was always the one wanting more animals, and he was always shooting me down. He was NEVER one to want another critter.

We brought the little guy home, and after several days of family arguing, we decided on the name Cubby.

Well, then the wreck happened, and some great friends took Cubby to their house for a few months while we dealt with the aftermath. He's been home for a couple of months now.

The thing is, Cubby is the best dog I've ever seen, and he's only eight months old. I feel like Tyler is laughing right now because the dog he chose is amazing and the dog I brought home unannounced five years ago is still a holy terror.

Today, I took Cubby to a local dog trainer who is going to train him to be a service dog for Weston. So, this dog, that never in a million years would I have imagined Tyler actually wanting, is going to be our boy's new bestie while he's in his chair and once he gets out of it.

Coincidentally, the trainer said he was the first car diverted around the wreck after it happened on his way back from a twenty-four-hour drive from Missouri.

God is good, and he always has plans for us.

November 14, 2021

A huge thank-you to Montana State Football for recognizing Tyler as their military hero at yesterday's game…where they came out on top of Idaho. Go Cats!

November 21, 2021

Happy Sunday!

Weston is doing amazing. On Friday, he went to his best buddy's birthday party. When I left, he was laughing, trash-talking, and doing normal eight-year-old boy stuff. It made my heart so happy.

On Friday, he also sat on a stool at PT by himself for a couple of minutes.

We finally heard back from Baltimore, and they're taking him in January. Their schedule was too full to get him in early, but God's timing is always the right timing. We'll keep plugging away here and working hard.

He's getting sassier and more obnoxious every day, which wears me out but also makes me grateful that he's getting back to him.

Prayers for his strength, perseverance, continued healing, and that his muscle tone improves so that we can do more to push him physically.

Wakes is doing great. She started seeing a therapist where she can talk about her daddy and brother, draw pictures, and write "poop." I think it's helping her a lot. She still thinks school is lame, but she has a big grin on her face every day when I pick her up.

Prayers for her continued healing and a thriving life.

Momma is doing better as well. I'm finally sleeping, thanks to antidepressants—it's so nice to wake up when my alarm goes off and not in the middle of the night.

I'm also putting this out there. I've been scared to talk about it, please don't judge. I think I'd like to start trying to meet a guy. I know it hasn't been a year yet, and I'm not desperate (yet), but, damn, it gets lonely. I have no idea how to do it because I've never had to, but I'm praying God puts the right guy in my life at the right time. A guy who can love me as fully as Tyler did, can love the kids like they deserve, loves Jesus, and enjoys doing all the epic stuff we love. He'll basically have to fall into my lap because my life revolves around the kids right now. A present father-figure was so important to Tyler, so I know he'd want someone around for the kids. They have amazing uncles and grandpas; it's just not the same as having someone always present.

We shall see what happens.

God is good.

November 25, 2021

I thought 2020 was a shitty year. I would complain about homeschooling (found out that was not my calling), and Tyler would tell me it wasn't all bad. He was grateful for the time we both had off work and the extra days we had the kids at home.

At Thanksgiving last year, we had to stay home quarantining and miss the big family get-together. So just the five of us celebrated and went out the next day to cut down a Christmas tree (Tyler insisted on a sixteen-footer, which we had to shorten up once we got home and realized it was too tall to stand). We got a couple of loads of wood, the kids adventured, it was great.

My point is, even when it seems like life is shitty, there's always something to be grateful for.

Even this year, which has been loads worse than 2020, has me thanking God every day.

Yes, I lost my boys too soon. But I'm grateful they both had the best lives I could hope for.

Tyler had a wife who loved him, kids who adored him, a job he was phenomenal at, and was blessed to travel to some fantastic places around the world and experience some pretty epic adventures.

Wyatt grew up in a loving home and was surrounded by a family who thought the world of him. He was fearless—on a steer (no matter how many times he got hurt), on his dirt bike, skiing, on the pitching mound, hunting gophers, lighting fires with his flint and steel, leading his pack of cousins. He truly loved life.

I am thankful that I will see them both again one day, and they'll say, "You lived a hell of a life."

Weston should not even be here, yet he is. I'm grateful for every word that comes out of his sassy little mouth, every time he tells me he's hungry, bored, or that I'm a crazy driver. I'm beyond thankful that he had his first voluntary muscle contractions at PT this week. His body is waking up! A miracle doesn't even begin to describe this boy. I'm thankful he inherited his daddy's fighting spirit and stubbornness, and that God has held him in his hand since the beginning.

I'm grateful my baby girl made it through with the fewest injuries of all, that every day she's coming back to her old self more and more, and that she continues to love her daddy and brothers so fiercely. I'm thankful for the unbelievable life I know she's going to live.

I'm grateful that my body has healed, my heart is getting there, and my soul is intact and not backing down. I'm thankful for all God has in store for the rest of my life.

I'm thankful for every single doctor who just happened to witness our wreck, the first responders who answered the call, the doctors and nurses who did everything they could for us, and the amazing rehab therapists we've all had to help us get back.

Lastly, I'm grateful for all the unbelievable people God has put in our lives. The blessings that were sent and continue to be sent our way. The friends I've gained who are now stuck with me for life (sorry). My family and Tyler's family came through for us in ways I never would've imagined—for them I will always be thankful. For each and every one of you and your unwavering support, thank you.

The year 2021 was a rough year for us, yet I still wrote a ridiculously long post about how thankful I am. Remember, there is good in every situation—you just have to be willing to see it. Have a blessed Thanksgiving.

God is good.

December 3, 2021

Over these last eight months, I've finally come to realize the true purpose of my life.

I've never had an easy life. There's been a lot of good, but also a lot of hard and flat-out shit. But I wouldn't ask for another one.

I've always kind of drifted through life with no real direction. In high school, I dabbled with the idea of becoming a doctor, considered sports medicine, got to college, and changed my major to animal science, then to biotechnology, and finally settled on exercise physiology because it sounded kind of cool.

I was accepted to grad school in MN for cardiac rehab, but the tall drink of water I was dating proposed and left for the military, so I headed back home to work for my basketball coach on his ranch for eighteen months (same place I worked during college and high school).

We got married and moved to AR, his duty station. We didn't particularly care for it, but we made the best of it for four years. While we were there, I realized a housewife was not my calling and decided to pursue my strength and conditioning certification and, in the meantime, fell into a freelance writing gig that continues to this day.

After AR, we transferred to MANG and moved to Great Falls. Found a house, Tyler worked on the hill, I continued writing and raising three kids (when Wakes was born, Wyatt had just turned three, and Wes was fifteen months—so it was insane).

The year Wy started kindergarten, Tyler deployed for five months. Left in October, came home in March, and I was totally on my own all winter with three little kids. Didn't know a soul in GF. But we made it. Actually, Tyler was gone a lot for work over the course of our marriage. He was off galivanting the globe, and I was here momming.

Five years ago, the school needed a gym teacher, so I decided to give it a whirl. Not a teacher, but I like exercise, so I went with it, haha. Three years ago, I took a chance and started an online health and fitness business. It's done wonderful.

Where am I going with all this babble? Despite the randomness and aimless direction my life seems to have taken, it has all prepared me for the here and now. To get through what has hit our family and help this little boy make a full recovery.

God did not orchestrate the wreck, but he knew it was coming and that I'd need every experience he could give me to make it through and bring GOOD out of it.

Growing up on a ranch, playing sports, doing hard manual labor jobs, experiencing my parents getting divorced, having poor self-esteem and a competitive nature, never knowing how things would work out, falling in love with lifting weights and ridiculous physical challenges. All of that has physically and mentally prepared me for what I'm doing now.

Tyler being gone so much prepared me for life as a truly single mom. Ranch work made me strong, independent, and gave me the ability to MacGyver any situation.

The natural ability I've always had to geek out over the human body, especially neurology, fascia, nutrition, and the muscular system, has allowed me to consume as much information as possible to help Weston. Not to mention the loads of information I already had in my brain.

My stubbornness, fighter's heart, and pigheadedness has also been a huge player in my life and continues to be. Thank you, God.

Finally, my knack for dreaming big—I've always wanted to open an in-person fitness space. But now the plan has shifted to a pediatric neuro-rehab facility here in GF. Ultimately, I believe that is what's supposed to come out of all this. Local help for families in our part of the country—not a single kid should ever slip between the cracks due to finances, lack of knowledge, or insufficient resources.

The fact that we have to go all the way to Baltimore is insane, as is the fact that I've had to do all the research to figure out how best to help Wes because the hospital sent us home with nothing. They had given up on him.

That is not acceptable; our kids deserve better. Our families deserve better.

Weston has essentially been the guinea pig, and I've been taking notes. Everything that has helped him will help others, which is what we love to do.

I don't know if any of this makes sense, but just know we will never be done with our work here until it's time for us to join our guys.

God is good.

December 7, 2021

We've already been blessed beyond my wildest dreams, yet there is more. A huge thank-you to our CCSAR commander for submitting our story to the amazing Tunnel to Towers Foundation. Our home was paid off in full today, the home Tyler and I built as our forever home two years ago.

Tyler always made sure we were taken care of when he was here, and, because of the selfless way he lived, he continues to do so.

God is good.

December 13, 2021

Happy Monday!

Just a super quick update—Weston starts his stint in Baltimore 01/10/22.

So excited to get him over there!

And the kids are stoked for Christmas.
Have an amazing week!
God is good.

December 24, 2021

Wishing you all a very Merry Christmas and a blessed New Year.

We are headed east on January 5, driving. The boy begins therapy on the tenth. I am so excited to get him over there. Tyler's mom is going over with me, and my mom is coming to stay with Wakely at our house. Our family is truly the best.

Wes had his first movement in lefty two days ago!

We went to a specialist eye doc on Tuesday in Missoula and got great news. There is very minimal sign of damage to the optic nerve; instead it seems to be an issue with processing and retrieving info rather than actual sight. His vision has already improved drastically, and now he makes eye contact when he talks to you. Bottom line, as God continues to knit his brain, his vision will continue to improve.

We miss our boys so much, but know they are here with us. I am so jealous they get to celebrate Christmas with the man himself.

Lastly, the kids are very excited for Christmas. Wakes said she only wanted a puppy or kitten (I told her hard no). Weston requested a dune buggy or another dirt bike (I told him when his legs wake up, we'll do some shopping).

Thank you all for all you have blessed us with. You are amazing, and we love you all.

God is good.

December 30, 2021

Okay, peeps, we need some serious prayers.

I got an email from Baltimore telling me that because of COVID, there was a possibility we would have to do telehealth instead of going into the clinic.

I'm sorry, but I am not driving across the country in the dead of winter to do telehealth appointments.

We have been waiting for next week for six months. Weston is so freakin' ready for this it's not even funny. We NEED to go. He NEEDS to get out of that damn chair.

I am not willing to accept that we now have to change our plans and wait longer because of a fucking little virus (pardon my language, but I am hot right now).

I'm asking each and every one of you to stop and pray right now that we are able to get the therapy this boy has been waiting for.

COVID is big, but my God is WAY BIGGER.

Weston has a lot to do with his life; he has already given everything and then some. He needs this, and he needs it now. Thank you.

God is good.

December 31, 2021

Just an update from the post yesterday.

I got to actually talk to Kennedy Krieger yesterday, and they assured me telehealth is not for sure but rather a possibility.

So instead of driving across the country for potential telehealth, we're going to postpone four to six weeks and then go over.

I emailed several facilities in surrounding states yesterday, just to see what I could find a little closer for the time being. I also have him set up to start hyperbaric treatment in Helena one to two times a week, starting next week.

His chiropractic care in Lewistown has been helping wake things up—his butt is always sore now from sitting in the chair. Left arm continues to improve. His brain is mending every single day.

Wakely is beautiful, intelligent, and such a wonderful sister to her brother. Their love for one another is amazing.

We miss our boys dearly but know they are so unbelievably happy.

We will be fine… God just likes to keep us on our toes.

Have a blessed New Year!

God is good.

January 2, 2022

I was taking the dogs for a walk this morning and couldn't help but think how much has changed in a year.

We had a really fabulous life. A wonderful, loving, crazy family. Everything was pretty freakin' great.

And then, literally, a blink of an eye changed everything.

I just want everyone to keep that in mind. To appreciate every single day. Don't waste a second. If you love someone, tell them. If you're pissed, say it.

Appreciate every experience and person that comes your way. Good or bad, it's an opportunity to become a better person.

Losing a spouse and son, as well as nearly losing my other two kids and my own life, has definitely given me a different perspective.

Life is short and unpredictable, even when you always do the right thing. So do it. Live it. Don't wait for tomorrow or next year. If it matters to you, do it now.

The three of us are going to keep pushing forward, living for the two who no longer get to and making the most out of what we've been given.

Don't wait for something horrible to change your life or to do something good. Goodness should always be your number one priority.

Do good. Live your life. Love.

God is good.

January 14, 2022

Cubby update. He is a stud, and he's killin' it.

Well done, Tyler John. You picked a good one.

January 20, 2022

Daddy-O Weir would've been thirty-six today.

Happy birthday, honey.

God, I wish you were here to celebrate your thirty-sixth year.

I never knew my heart could hurt so bad.

You were too full of life to be gone so early.

The world is lesser without you, your big ol' grin, your sweet dance moves, your smart-ass comments, random knowledge bombs, and your grit.

You had a beautiful soul, and your love for life is something I aspire to.

I hope you and Wy party hard up there today—if I could, I'd be skiing for you today.

We miss you every single day.

Thank you for loving us so hard.

Happy birthday, baby.

I love you,

Me

January 26, 2022

Okay, update time.

Today finds us in Spokane. We came over yesterday with plans to check in to St. Luke's pediatric rehab—it was supposed to be a surprise; we got the call on Tyler's birthday.

When we were about thirty minutes away from my in-laws', we got a call. St. Luke's is no longer accepting new rehab patients because they have to make room for COVID patients. I called and told them we were already here; they said we'd have to wait a few weeks.

By now, you all know that's not really my thing.

I cried and went for a run. When I was running, I was praying for guidance of what to do next.

Do you know what came to me?

COVID = Satan

So now I get to share that with you. Yes, COVID has impacted all of us in a negative way for obvious reasons. But think about it, what else has come along and divided us like it has?

Family members disowning one another, people not getting the health care they need, fighting over masks (I recently watched a video of a young woman verbally and physically assaulting an elderly gentleman on a plane because he took his mask off to eat—she had hers off the entire time she attacked him), vaccine mandates, people having to choose between their means of supporting their family and complying with these mandates, our military losing thousands of experienced service members; the country is divided.

The real reason we didn't go to Chicago is because they wanted me to get vaccinated; we would've then had to quarantine for ten days, and then they would give us ten days of therapy.

That is absolutely not acceptable. They held my son's care hostage with my vaccination status. I told them absolutely not.

There are lines I will not cross.

Everyone is allowed to have their own beliefs, but don't you dare tell me what I HAVE to do.

Satan has been quite busy stirring the COVID pot, and he's doing a very good job. He's doing his best to put these roadblocks up for us to make my faith falter. Unfortunately for him, I have God, Jesus, the Holy Spirit, Tyler, and Wyatt in my corner. The ol' devil doesn't stand a chance.

Today, I told him he can go ahead and go back to hell where he belongs because there is absolutely nothing he can do to stop us. We have work today, and he's making it a real pain in the ass to get it done.

My God is bigger than Satan, he's bigger than any injury, any diagnosis, any circumstance.

Good will prevail, and the devil and COVID can kiss my ass.

I'm currently calling a few other places in town—God brought us to Spokane for a reason, devil be damned.

God is good.

February 1, 2022

A quick sitrep on the Weir front.

We are still in Spokane, waiting for St. Luke's to call with the go-ahead. In the meantime, we're getting lots of family time—we went and visited Tyler's G'ma Ann the other day. One of my absolute favorite ladies.

We were hooked up with a small clinic in Deer Park for PT (coincidentally Deer Park is very close to the lake cabin, the boys' favorite place in the world—thank you, King Lion, for continuing to take care of your family).

I forgot to mention, Wes had received twelve hyperbaric treatments in Great Falls before we left, and they were already making a difference.

Wakes is at home with Meemaw. Going to school and living the dream. The kids miss each other a lot, but they are both hanging in there.

I have fully turned everything over to God. Life is beyond my control, but he's got it. Always has.

Please continue to send up prayers for these kids. They have a big life planned for them.

I feel like a lot of people have considered me a little crazy for a long time. From the doctors in Seattle to people at home who look at me funny when I say Wes is doing amazing.

You know what? I am a little crazy. I'm even crazier now than I was before the wreck. You know why? Because I didn't die. I'm still here. I have a lot to do. I don't have time for fear. I don't have time for bullshit. I only have time to do what God has called me to do. Go big or go home.

If we choose to live a small life, we do not make enough room for a big God.

My God is big.

My God is good.

February 6, 2022

Happy Sunday!

I hope everyone had a great weekend. Wes and I are getting some great family time in over in Spokane.

Thursday, as I lay down to pray (and possibly nap) to officially and finally give EVERYTHING over to God, I realized I've done all I can do as a crazy human.

St. Luke's called while I was in slumberland and left me a message. Since I was finally able to request an outpatient, they thought they could make it happen!

Inpatient was going to be at least another month, and, honestly, neither one of us would have fared well cooped up in the hospital. If for some reason this falls through, Shriners said they would be able to take him.

I would also like to say that despite how horrible this last year has been, it's also been amazing.

Yes, we miss our boys every single day, but so much good and blessings have come as well.

We've met so many amazing people, I've gained friends I could not live without, we've had more prayers sent up on our behalf (I have a feeling I'm going to get "the look" from God when I finally get home), I've had the privilege of witnessing so many miracles that the right words elude me, we've learned you can handle so much more than you can possibly fathom, I've had some pretty serious tasks put on my heart, and we've learned what's really important in life—how we need to continue LIVING, laughing, and loving every single day.

Thank you all, for everything.

God is good.

February 13, 2022

Weston James is finally starting some rehab!

After the whole COVID debacle, I requested outpatient with St. Luke's. We waited for two weeks and then were able to get evals done.

Normally, they only see patients a couple of times per week, but they're really working hard to get him in with all three therapists as often as possible. Last week, he did all three—OT, ST, and PT back-to-back Thursday and Friday. He was a smoked little bear.

The therapists are amazing and focus on brain injury therapy as opposed to general therapy.

On Thursday, he identified the colored cones he had to find around the room. He did it perfectly—first time since the wreck! So now we know for sure his color vision is still intact.

He dances at the house and at therapy. He's connived his therapists into letting him listen to Jon Pardi while he works, but then he gets too busy dancing to do what he's supposed to do.

Despite all this kid has been through, he has the best attitude I have ever seen. We're still working hard on getting his confidence up so that he believes he can do everything again.

He's been getting lots of nana and papa time in and wines (tequila and whiskey too; Nana and he have a drinking game with Jon Pardi songs—works great to keep him hydrated!) all the time— last two pictures.

God is good.

February 23, 2022

Hello, friends!

I figured I should probably pop in and let you know we're still kicking over here in Spokane.

The therapists are amazing and focusing on neuro rehab tactics for the boy.

We're not doing five days per week, which was the inpatient plan, but they're getting him in as often as possible.

I just got in contact with another therapy place here that uses MNRI (Masgutova Neurosensorimotor Reflex Integration)—essentially it helps rewire his brain, neurons, and nerves. I'm praying that will be a good supplement to what he's doing at St. Luke's.

He's improving every single day and has even begun grieving for his daddy and brother. It breaks my heart but makes me so happy that he's starting to process his loss.

Wakes is crushing first grade, and likely her teacher's soul. But it is what it is. She's a little champ hanging with Meemaw.

Lastly, Momma is doing well. I think the entire reason we ended up in Spokane outpatient and not inpatient, not Baltimore, not Chicago, and not Arizona, is because this is where we're supposed to be.

We're staying with Tyler's mom, which has given me help and the opportunity to get outside for long jaunts every day. But mostly it has given me the time I needed to fully work through my grief. I've had to be Momma since the second I woke up. It has been all about the kids. Now my soul finally has time to heal and rest. Thank you, Jesus, and thank you, Nana.

Please be ferocious with your spirit and pray for this little dude, that his brain and body are fully restored and that he finds the courage and will to WANT to get out of that chair. Thank you.

God is good.

March 4, 2022

Weston is slaying life. I ran home last week and grabbed Wakes to come spend a long weekend with us. They had fun together and argued.

Uncle Ryan and Uncle Mikey (Tyler's best friends) took us bowling last weekend. Wes would use the force to charge the ball before I rolled it for him. He actually came in right behind his uncles.

He's doing great at therapy, hit the new therapy place yesterday for PT—I'm excited to see what they can do with him.

I'm praying another month here will get him over the hump so we can head home and continue working there.

Every single person that meets Wes knows his favorite singer is Jon Pardi—he insists on listening to it at therapy because it helps him work better…and poor Alexa is sick and tired of him yelling at her. Anyhoo, I just found out Mr. Pardi is going to be in Spokane in July, so I snagged some tickets for us to go. I just hope he likes him as much in person as he does on my phone.

Lastly, we are so grateful to get to spend this time with Nana and Papa Randy while we're here. We truly have the best family.

God is good.

March 15, 2022

So, Weston is doing pretty dang good. He's getting more leg movement every day, his memory is improving, and his muscle tone is diminishing daily!

We've got a couple of more weeks in Spokane, then we're headed back home to continue the push forward.

After the last post about Wes's favorite music man, an amazing guy from Great Falls messaged me that he went to high school with Mr. Pardi, so he reached out to Pardi's sister, who is awesome!

She loved the videos of Wes and arranged for the little dude to get a box of swag, which arrived last Friday. He was absolutely stoked about it. He has one of his new tees on in the pic. People are the best!

God is good.

March 27, 2022

All men die, but not all men live.

Thank God you both lived. And lived well.

This last year has been a heck of a ride.

There has been a lot of pain and a whole lotta darkness.

But there has also been so much dang good.

You boys carried so much light through your lives, when you left, it had no choice but to carry on.

I miss you every day, but the hurt doesn't hit me in the gut and take me to my knees anymore.

It's just my constant companion to remind me how much I loved you, and you me.

You'd both be so proud of Wes and Wakes; they're carrying on the tradition.

You boys keep ridin' high, and don't forget to check in on us every once in a while.

Love,

Me

April 8, 2022

We are back home!

Spokane was amazing; the therapists there did so much good work with Weston.

We are getting back to work here in Great Falls, and the boy is going to school in the mornings. He loves being with his classmates and seeing his buddies.

Weston and Wakes are both in soccer this spring. Wakes played her first game last weekend and loved it! Wes hasn't made a practice or a game yet, but he got to see his teammates yesterday for picture day. They were all pretty wound up.

We are home, we are happy, we are blessed.

God is good.

April 17, 2022

HE IS RISEN.

Happy Easter from these hooligans!

Kids are good.

Mom is good.

God is good.

April 23, 2022

Weston's tablet made this little video the other day, and I had to share it.

I forget the progress he has made because I see him every day.

But, oh my, that boy has come so far.

I just watched the video post I did a year ago this morning for him. I spoke about how the doctors had zero hope for him, how he was having a shunt put in his head, and how he showed his first bit of emotion when they cleaned the goo out of his hair. He had looked me in the eye and cried while they did it. Today he looks me in the eye and either cusses or tells me he loves me.

This little boy is an amazing miracle, and I'm so grateful I get to witness it every day.

And the people in our lives... Lord, we are blessed.

God is good.

May 1, 2022

God's timing is always the perfect timing.

Today this handsome boy was confirmed into the Catholic Church and received First Communion, something he's been looking forward to for the last two years.

It was a beautiful day; my heart was full and happy.

God is good.

May 4, 2022

Cubby came home last week; it was amazing to have him home.

Unfortunately, working with him and getting Weston all over was too much for me.

The trainers graciously agreed to take him home for a bit longer to keep working with him until I can get my poop in a group and make the time he deserves.

All I can say to them is thank you. They worked hard with our boy over the last seven months, and I'm so excited to put him to work. When we went to get him, they hooked a rope up to the wheelchair, and Weston got to "mush" Cubs—he thought it was fantastic!

Thank you, North Pack K9 LLC, for the amazing work you do and all the attention you give our special guy.

God is good.

May 17, 2022

Hey, folks! Just wanted to drop in for a quick.

Wes has been busy doing some sort of therapy every single day.

We go to Ft. Benton twice a week so he can spend some time in the Moon Walker (some friends sent me an article from KRTV about another little boy who was using it—so, of course, I got Weston over there).

He complains a lot, ha ha, but today I stayed out of sight while he worked, minus the video part, and he just chatted with Mr. Gage and did his work.

Still waiting on that miracle of walking, but I know it will come when God and the boy are ready for it.

Wakes has a couple weeks of school left until FREEEEEEEEDOM!

Mom is alive.

God is good.

May 27, 2022

This popped up today, and I can't begin to tell you how fitting it is.

Today, I need to give thanks to God.

This boy.

Yesterday at PT in Ft. Benton, the therapist called me to come back at the end of the session. Why? Because Weston's left leg was gliding oh so smoothly when the PT moved it forward. Not only was it moving freely, it also felt as though Weston was helping it move. It was very minor, but boy was I happy about it.

This morning when I went to get him up, his left AFO (braces he wears on his ankles at night) was completely off. These things fit VERY snugly and are Velcroed on with two straps. I have to work to get them off every day. I asked how the heck he managed to get it off, and he told me he had a dream about running a marathon. I'm still not sure how it came off, but he must've been moving like crazy.

Once he was dressed, I sat him up to sit on the edge of the bed while I put his shoes on. We do this every morning—he sits 100 percent on his own.

This morning, he told me he was going back to bed. (He does this a lot now that he realized he could safely lay himself back down. Then I have to sit him back up.) I told him to wait until I was done getting his shoes on, but, of course, he didn't listen.

He went back. I told him to sit up. And he did! I woohooed for him and told him to do it again.

Four times, he lay down and then sat himself up to sitting! I yelled for Wakes, and she went to get her tablet so she could video him, but by then he was too tired to do it again.

To some these may seem minor, but to his momma who has been going and going every day with no reprieve, these are huge. I have been praying so hard all week for God to help us along, and then we get these little miracles.

I continue to pray for Weston to overcome his fears and have the confidence he needs to keep pushing forward. My boy will walk.

I am so grateful I stuck with my faith and didn't let the doctor's prognosis diminish it, no matter how bleak they proposed his future would be.

God is always in control.

God always works for our good.

God is good.

Post from last year

Okay, it's time for a real-life Weston update. I have been going back and forth about sharing these, but I've had an overwhelming urge to let you all know that the POWER OF PRAYER IS REAL.

The first picture is the first time I saw Weston after the wreck in the first week of April. Our boy was in very rough shape.

He had five broken bones, multiple rib fractures, blood on his lungs, a ruptured spleen, and a severe traumatic brain injury. Probably some stuff I'm missing.

The picture of him looking at the camera was from last week and taken by amazing friends who volunteered to go stay with him while we all came home for the funerals.

The last one of him in the helmet was taken Tuesday by my mother-in-law, who flew straight back to Seattle after the funeral.

That's right, on Tuesday, my boy sat on the edge of his bed! The first time he has not been lying flat on his back in the last almost nine weeks.

I've had so many people ask me how Weston is, and when I tell them he's improving every single day, they look at me like I'm a crazy person who's lost her grip with reality.

But I need every one of you to know that my beautiful boy is a miracle who is only beginning to show us what he's capable of. Weston is going to move mountains, of that I am certain.

So what I need to say is:

Prayer is powerful.

God is good.

My baby is healing every day.

Please keep praying; y'all are doing more for us then you can possibly imagine.

June 22, 2022

Heya! It's been quite a while since we chatted.

All is well here.

Kids are enjoying summer. We're busy going to therapy every single day, but it gets us out of the house.

We've managed to get PT four times per week, twice with Benefis and twice in Ft. Benton. He gets OT and speech once per week.

Weston is finally asking to go outside and play. He keeps asking to go help me do chores too, which we can't really do with the wheelchair, but it makes me so happy that he's getting interested in doing stuff outside again.

Playing catch is his favorite, and he's pretty darn good at it.

Wakes is enjoying her wild woman lifestyle and manages to find things to keep her busy—including fighting with Weston.

Mom is maintaining her sanity…kind of.

Next week, I'm starting a nine-month life coaching program so that I can use our experience for more good and help anyone I can.

I've also started researching how to get the book published. It's been in the works since last fall, not finished yet but will be as soon as God tells me to wrap it up.

We made it through Wyatt's eleventh birthday on May 31. It hit me super hard this year; last year I was still pretty out of it. But I made it through, and the fifth-grade class at the school planted a beautiful tree in his memory.

We celebrated Father's Day by taking a Batman figurine to the cemetery—the first time Tyler TDY'd, I put it in his bathroom bag. He packed it everywhere with him for nine years; now Batman stands guard for the boys.

I hope everyone is having an amazing summer!

God is good.

July 14, 2022

One year ago, yesterday, Weston came home.

It amazes me how far he has come and how far he will go.

When he came home, he couldn't eat, speak, or make any meaningful movements, and could only look to the right—eyes and head.

Today, he talks nonstop, feeds himself, plays catch, plays with his toys, paints, fights with his sister, argues with me, leans out of his chair, and looks wherever the heck he wants, and yesterday he had purposeful movement in both legs—he kicked a soccer ball at PT!

His left arm is getting more and more relaxed; movement will be there soon.

A year is long time, but it's a very short time when you consider how much healing this boy has received.

Here's to the next year of miracles.

God is good.

August 4, 2022

Big guy is consistently progressing every day.

We've been practicing this bend and straighten exercise every morning for the last week. As long as his heels don't hang up in the bed, he can move BOTH legs.

Yesterday, he shot hoops at PT…while he was kneeling on the floor, activating those glutes and spinal extensors.

He was "running" in his wheelchair yesterday—his right arm was driving up and down, and lefty was moving too.

I'd like to thank all the therapists we've worked with over the last year. Every single one has fully committed to the process of getting Wes up and running again. You've all been amazing.

Thank you also to those individuals who have taken the time to come up and work on school stuff with Wes, paint, play, or just chat.

He has reached the point where he is no longer content sitting and playing his tablet. He wants to go on walks, help with chores, play catch, you name it. I'm so happy that he's no longer okay with being confined to his chair. He's been needing that fuel to keep working.

Oh, and Cubby came home yesterday! Thank you, North Pack K9 LLC, for taking such good care of our boy and making him into one darn good mutt.

Never give up on what you want.

Prayer is powerful. God is good.

August 24, 2022

The turd burglars had their first day of school today!

Wakes is in second grade.

Weston is doing third and fourth. The school is doing an awesome job getting him in there, and an amazing woman who retired from teaching last spring offered to be his personal assistant this year. She's a saint.

Therapy is going fantastic, and the kidney stones that Seattle was so worried about are completely gone.

God is good.

For more baby steps, please visit the Weir Family Warriors on Facebook.

Conclusion

It's been eighteen months since Tyler and Wyatt left us. There are days I still can't believe they're gone. They were both bigger than life and so full of good and goofiness, it's hard to fathom life without them.

There are still days (like this morning) where their loss hits me like a freight train. I cry, pray, meditate, run, and talk to them. They both loved me unconditionally, no matter how crazy I got. I miss their hugs, their laughs, their smart-aleck remarks. I miss Tyler's big ol' arms wrapping around me and Wyatt calling me Momma. My soul still aches, my heart still hurts, my body still craves their presence.

I miss the Weston and Wakely I knew before the wreck. However, I can't linger on that grief because I am even more grateful they're both still here with me. The kids they are becoming amaze me. They're different, yes, but so am I. We've all stood at the abyss and come back to live the best lives we can. It hasn't been easy, but it has been good. I thank God every day I hear them goofing, fighting, and laughing. All are sweet, sweet sounds to a Momma who has had to say goodbye to a baby and who could have lost so much more.

I wrote this book to show that even when life gets really bad, there will always be good to find if you're willing to look for it. A tragic event happened in our lives; rather than playing the victims, we're trying to bring as much good out of it as we possibly can. I am grateful for every single day and every circumstance I find myself in.

These last eighteen months have been the most difficult of my entire life. Yet every single day I wake up and press forward. Even though I have completely changed as a person, my faith has never wavered. I have lived by a phrase Tyler used regularly: "Hooyah, never quit." I haven't, and I will not.

I know that where there should have been five casualties, there were only two. Why? I'm not entirely sure yet, but I do know God has a plan for each of us. I trust him entirely and believe I still have many very happy years left to experience in my life.

I know that prayer is the most powerful weapon available to us. Every time a prayer was uttered on our behalf, it was an arrow directly targeting doubt and fear, neither of which we've ever had time for. I am grateful for each and every person who has taken the time to pray for my family; we wouldn't be here without you. It was honestly a team effort.

It doesn't matter what life throws your way; if you're willing to keep moving forward, nothing can stop you. You can do all things through Christ and your own will and determination. We are living proof of that.

Don't dwell on the bad, the negative, or what you can't control. Focus on faith, the good, and what you can do to help yourself make forward progress. Every little step moves you in the right direction until you look back and can't believe how far you've come.

Life is hard, but God is good.

About the Author

Jen Weir is a survivor, alive today because her work here is not finished. She's at home in Montana with her two miracle kids and the family God knew she would need. Jen serves in each and every capacity that is put on her heart. Parenting, writing, speaking, and health and life coaching are currently at the top of the list. She doesn't know where life is going to take her, but she trusts it will be good.

Printed in the USA
CPSIA information can be obtained
at www.ICGtesting.com
LVHW050906240823
755926LV00004B/469